HENRY GEORGE

THE

IRISH LAND QUESTION

What it Involves, and how alone it can be Settled

Elibron Classics
www.elibron.com

Elibron Classics series.

ISBN 1-4021-6279-0 (paperback)
ISBN 1-4212-8032-9 (hardcover)

This Elibron Classics Replica Edition is an unabridged facsimile of the edition published in 1881 by Cameron & Ferguson, London.

"We hold these truths to be self-evident: That all men are created equal; that they are endowed by their Creator with certain inalienable rights; that among these are life, liberty, and the pursuit of happiness. That to secure these rights, governments are instituted among men, deriving their just powers from the consent of the governed; that, whenever any form of government becomes destructive of these ends, it is the right of the people to alter or to abolish it."—DECLARATION OF INDEPENDENCE.

THE

IRISH LAND QUESTION:

What it Involves, and how alone it can be Settled.

AN APPEAL TO THE LAND LEAGUES.

BY

HENRY GEORGE,

AUTHOR OF "PROGRESS AND POVERTY."

Contents.

LONDON:

CAMERON & FERGUSON, SALISBURY SQUARE.

GLASGOW: WEST NILE STREET.

PRICE 1881. SIXPENCE

THE

IRISH LAND QUESTION.

I.

In charging the Dublin jury in the Land League cases, Mr Justice Fitzgerald told them that the land laws of Ireland were more favourable to the tenant than those of Great Britain, Belgium, or the United States.

As a matter of fact, Justice Fitzgerald is right. For in Ireland certain local customs and the provisions of the Bright Land Act mitigate somewhat the power of the landlord in his dealings with the tenant. In Great Britain, save by custom in a few localities, there are no such mitigations. In Belgium I believe there are none. There are certainly none in the United States.

This fact which Justice Fitzgerald cites will be re-echoed by the enemies of the Irish movement. And it is a fact well worth the consideration of its friends. For the Irish movement has passed its first stage, and it is time for a more definite understanding of what is needed and how it is to be got.

It is the fashion of Land League orators and sympathising newspapers in this country to talk as if the distress and disquiet in Ireland were caused by British oppression, and our National House of Representatives recently passed by unanimous vote a resolution which censured England for her treatment of Ireland. But, while it is true that in the past Ireland has been deeply wronged and bitterly oppressed by England, it is not true that there is—in an economic sense, at least—any peculiar oppression of Ireland by England now. To whatever cause Irish distress may be due, it is certainly not due to any English laws which press on industry more heavily in Ireland than in any other part of the United Kingdom.

And, further than this, the Irish land system, which is so much talked of as though it were some peculiarly atrocious system, is essentially the same land system which prevails in all civilised countries, which we of the United States have accepted unquestioningly, and have extended over the whole temperate zone of a new continent—the same system which all over the civilised world men are accustomed to consider natural and just.

Justice Fitzgerald is unquestionably right.

As to England, it is well known that the English landlords exercise freely all the powers complained of in the Irish landlords, without even the slight restrictions imposed in Ireland.

As to Belgium, let me quote the high authority of the distinguished Belgian publicist, M. Emile de Laveleye, of the University of Liege. He says that the Belgian tenant-farmers —for tenancy largely prevails even where the land is most minutely divided—are rack-rented with a mercilessness unknown in England or even in Ireland, and are compelled to vote as their landlords dictate!

And as to the United States, let me ask the men who to applauding audiences are nightly comparing the freedom of America with the oppression of Ireland—let me ask the Representatives who voted for that resolution of sympathy with Ireland, this simple question: What would the Irish landlords lose, what would the Irish tenants gain, if, to-morrow, Ireland were made a State in the American Union and American law substituted for English law?

I think it will puzzle them to reply. The truth is that the gain would be to the landlords, the loss to the tenants. The simple truth is, that, under our laws, the Irish landlords could rack-rent, distrain, evict, or absent themselves, as they pleased, and without any restriction from Ulster tenant-right or legal requirement of compensation for improvements. Under our laws they could, just as freely as they can now, impose whatever terms they pleased upon their tenants—whether as to cultivation, as to improvements, as to game, as to marriages, as to voting, or as to anything else. For these powers do not spring from special laws. They are merely incident to the right of property; they result simply from the acknowledgment of the right of the owner of land to do as he pleases with his own—to let it, or not let it. So far as law can give them to him, every American landlord has these powers as fully as any Irish landlord. Can not the American owner of land make, in letting it, any stipulation he pleases as to how it shall be used, or improved, or cultivated? Can he not reserve any of his own rights upon it, such as the right of entry, or of cutting wood, or shooting game, or catching fish? And, in the absence of special agreement, does not American law give him, what, as I understand it, the law of Ireland does not now give him, the ownership at the expiration of the lease of all the improvements made by the tenant?

What single power has the Irish landowner that the American landowner has not as fully? Is not the American landlord just as free as is the Irish landlord to refuse to rent his lands or his houses to any one who does not attend a certain church or vote a certain ticket? Is he not quite as free to do this as he is free to refuse his contributions to all but one particular benevolent society or political committee? Or, if, not liking a certain newspaper, he chooses to give notice to quit to any tenant whom he finds taking that newspaper, what law can be invoked to prevent him? There is none. The property is his, and he can let it or not let it, as he wills. And, having this power to let or not let, he has power to demand any terms he pleases.

That Ireland is a conquered country; that centuries ago her soil was taken from its native possessors and parcelled out among aliens, and that it has been confiscated again and again, has nothing to do with the real question of to-day—no more to do with it than have the confiscations of Marius and Sylla. England, too, is a conquered country; her soil has been confiscated again and again; and, spite of all talk about the Saxon oppressor and the down-trodden Celt, it is not probable that, after the admixture of generations, the division of landholder and non-landholder any more coincides with distinction of race in the one country than in the other. That Irish land titles rest on force and fraud is true; but so do land titles in every country—even to a large extent in our own peacefully settled country. Even in our most recently settled States, how much land is there to which title has been got by fraud and perjury and bribery—by the arts of the lobbyist or the cunning tricks of hired lawyers, by double-barreled shot-guns and repeating rifles!

The truth is that the Irish land system is simply the general system of modern civilization. In no essential feature does it differ from the system that obtains here—in what we are accustomed to consider the freest land under the sun. Entails and primogeniture and family settlements may be in themselves bad things, and may sometimes interfere with putting the land to its best use, but their effects upon the relations of landlord and tenant are not worth talking about. As for rack-rent, which is simply a rent fixed at short intervals by competition, that is in the United States even a more common way of letting land than in Ireland. In our cities the majority of our people live in houses rented from month to month or year to year for the highest price the landlord thinks he can get. The usual term, in the newer States, at least, for the letting of agricultural land is from season to season. And that the rent of land in the United States comes, on the whole, more closely to the standard of rack, or full competition rent, there can be, I think, little doubt. That the land of Ireland is, as the apologists for landlordism say, largely under-rented (that is, not rented for the full amount the landlord might get with free competition) is probably true. Miss C. G. O'Brien, in a recent article in the "Nineteenth Century," states that the tenant-farmers generally get for such patches as they sublet to their labourers twice the rent they pay the landlords. And we hear incidentally of many "good landlords," i.e., landlords not in the habit of pushing their tenants for as much as they might get by vigorously demanding all that any one would give.

These things, as well as the peculiar bitterness of complaints against middle-men and the speculators who have purchased encumbered estates and manage them solely with a view to profit, go to show the truth of the statement that the land of Ireland has been, by its present owners, largely underlet, when considered from what we would deem a business point of view. And this is but what might be expected. Human nature is about the same the world over, and the Irish landlords as a class are no better nor worse than would be other men under like conditions. An aristocracy such as that of Ireland has its virtues as well as its vices, and is influenced by sentiments which do not enter into mere business transactions—sentiments which must often modify and soften the calculations of cold self-interest. But with us the letting of land is as much a business matter as the buying or selling of pig-iron or of stocks. An American would not think he was showing his goodness by renting his land for low rates, any more than he would think he was showing his goodness by selling pig-iron for less than the market price, or stocks for less than the quotations. So in those districts of France and Belgium where the land is most subdivided, the peasant proprietors, says M. de Laveleye, boast to one another of the high rents they get, just as they boast of the high prices they get for pigs or for poultry.

The best measure of rent is, of course, its proportion to the produce. The only estimate of Irish rent as a proportion of which I know is that of Buckle, who puts it at one fourth of the produce. In this country I am inclined to think one fourth would generally be considered a moderate rent. Even in California there is considerable land rented for one third the crop, and some that rents for one half the crop; while, according to a writer in the "Atlantic Monthly," the common rent in that great wheat-growing section of the new North-west now being opened up is one half the crop!

It does not seem to me that Justice Fitzgerald's statement can be disputed. The American land system is really worse for the tenant than the Irish system. For with us there is neither sentiment nor custom to check the force of competition or mitigate the natural desire of the landlord to get all he can.

Nor is there anything in our system to prevent or check absenteeism, so much complained of in regard to Ireland. Before the modern era, which has so facilitated travel and communication, and made the great cities so attractive to those having money to spend, the prevalence of Irish absenteeism may have been due to special causes, but at the present day there is certainly nothing peculiar in it. Most of the large English and Scotch landholders are absentees for the greater part of the year, and many of them live permanently or for long intervals upon the Continent. So are our large American landowners generally absentees. In New York, in San Francisco, in Washington, Boston, Chicago, and St Louis, live men who own large tracts of land which they seldom or never see. A resident of Rochester is said to own no less than four hundred farms in different States, one of which (I believe in Kentucky) comprises thirty-five thousand acres. Under the plantation system of farming and that of stock-raising on a grand scale, which are developing so rapidly in our new States, very much of the profits go to professional men and capitalists who live in distant cities. Corporations whose stock is held in the East or in Europe own much greater bodies of land, at much greater distances, than do the London corporations possessing landed estates in Ireland. To say nothing of the great land-grant railroad companies, the Standard Oil Company probably owns more acres of Western land than all the London companies put together own of Irish land. And, although landlordism in its grosser forms is only beginning in the United States, there is probably no American, wherever he may live, who cannot in his immediate vicinity see some instance of absentee landlordism. The tendency to concentration born of the new era ushered in by the application of steam shows itself in this way as in many others. To those who can live where they please, the great cities are becoming more and more attractive.

And it is further to be remarked that the evils of absenteeism are much exaggerated. That is to say, that to his tenantry and neighbourhood the owner of land in Galway or Kilkenny would be as much an absentee if he lived in Dublin as if he lived in London, and that, if Irish landlords were compelled to live in Ireland, all that the Irish people would gain would be, metaphorically speaking, the crumbs that fell from the landlords' tables. For if the butter and eggs, the pigs and the poultry, of the Irish peasant must be taken from him and exported to pay for his landlord's wine and cigars, what difference does it make to him where the wine is drunk or the cigars are smoked?

II.

But it will be asked: If the land system which prevails in Ireland is essentially the same as that which prevails elsewhere, how is it that it does not produce the same results elsewhere?

I answer that it does everywhere produce the same *kind* of results. As there is nothing essentially peculiar in the Irish land system, so is there nothing essentially peculiar in Irish distress. Between the distress in Ireland and the distress in other countries there may be differences in degree and differences in manifestation; but that is all.

The truth is, that as there is nothing peculiar in the Irish land system, so is there nothing peculiar in the distress which that land system causes. We hear a great deal of Irish emigration, of the millions of sons and daughters of Erin who have been compelled to leave their native soil. But have not the Scottish Highlands been all but depopulated? Do not the English emigrate in the same way, and for the same reasons? Do not the Germans and Italians and Scandinavians also emigrate? Is there not a constant emigration from the Eastern States of the Union to the Western—an emigration impelled by the same motives as that which sets across the Atlantic? Nor am I sure that this is not in some respects a more demoralising emigration than the Irish, for I do not think there is any such monstrous disproportion of the sexes in Ireland as in Massachusetts? If French and Belgian peasants do not emigrate as do the Irish, is it not simply because they do not have such "long families?"

There has been recently deep and wide-spread distress in Ireland, and but for the contributions of charity many of her people would have perished for want of food. But, to say nothing of such countries as India, China, Persia, and Syria, is it not true that within the last few years there have been similar spasms of distress in the most highly civilized countries

—not merely in Russia and in Poland, but in Germany and England? Yes, even in the United States.

Have there not been, are there not constantly occurring, in all these countries, times when the poorest classes are reduced to the direst straits, and large numbers are only saved from starvation by charity.

When there is famine among savages it is because food enough is not to be had. But this was not the case in Ireland. In any part of Ireland, during the height of what was called the famine, there was food enough for whoever had means to pay for it. The trouble was not in the scarcity of food. There was, as a matter of fact, no real scarcity of food, and the proof of it is that food did not command scarcity prices. During all the so-called famine, food was constantly exported from Ireland to England, which would not have been the case had there been any more true famine in the one country than in the other. During all the so-called famine a practically unlimited supply of American meat and grain could, through the existing mechanism of exchange, have been poured into Ireland so quickly that the relief would have been felt instantaneously. Our sending of supplies in a national war-ship was a piece of vulgar ostentation, fitly paralleled by their ostentatious distribution in British gunboats, under the nominal superintendence of a royal prince. Had we been bent on relief, not display, we might have saved our Government the expense of fitting up its antiquated war-ship, the British gunboats their coal, the Lord Mayor his dinner, and the royal prince his valuable time. A cable draft, turned in Dublin into postal orders, would have afforded the relief, not merely much more easily and cheaply, but in less time than it took our war-ship to get ready to receive her cargo; for the reason that so many of the Irish people were starving was—not that the food was not to be had, but that they had not the means to buy it. Had the Irish people had money or its equivalent, the bad seasons might have come and gone without stinting any one of a full meal. Their effect would merely have been to determine toward Ireland the flow of more abundant harvests.

I wish clearly to bring to view this point. The Irish famine was not a true famine arising from the scarcity of food. It was what an English writer styled the Indian famine—a "financial famine," arising not from scarcity of food, but from the poverty of the people. The effect of the short crops in producing distress was not so much in raising the price of food as in cutting off the accustomed incomes of the people. The masses of the Irish people get so little in ordinary times that they are barely able to live, and when anything occurs to interrupt their accustomed incomes, they have nothing to fall back on.

Yet is this not true of large classes in all countries? And are not all countries subject to just such famines as this Irish famine? Good seasons and bad seasons are in the order of nature, just as the day of sunshine and the day of rain, the summer's warmth and the winter's snow. But agriculture is, on the whole, as certain as any other pursuit, for even those industries which may be carried on regardless of weather are subject to alternations as marked as those to which agriculture is liable. There are good seasons and bad seasons even in fishing and hunting, while the alternations are very marked in mining and in manufacturing. In fact, the more highly differentiated branches of industry which advancing civilization tends to develop, though less directly dependent upon rain and sunshine, heat and cold, seem increasingly subject to alternations more frequent and intense. Though in a country of more diversified industry, the failure of a crop or two could not have such widespread effects as in Ireland, yet the countries of more complex industries are liable to a greater variety of disasters. A war on another continent produces famine in Lancashire; Parisian milliners decree a change of fashion, and Coventry operatives are only saved from starvation by public alms; a railroad combination decides to raise the price of coal, and Pennsylvania miners find their earnings diminished by half, or totally cut off; a bank breaks in New York, and in all the large American cities soup-houses must be opened!

In this Irish famine which provoked the land agitation, there is nothing that is peculiar. Such famines on a smaller or a larger scale are constantly occurring. Nay, more, the fact is, that famine—just such famine as this Irish famine—constantly exists in the richest and most highly civilized lands. It persists even in "good times" when trade is "booming;" it spreads and rages whenever from any cause industrial depression comes. It is kept under—or, at least, kept from showing its worst phases—by poor rates and almshouses, by private benevolence, and by vast organised charities, but it still exists, gnawing in secret when it does not openly rage. In the very centres of civilization, where the machinery of production and exchange is at the highest point of efficiency—where bank-vaults hold millions, and show-windows flash with more than a prince's ransom, where elevators and warehouses are gorged with grain, and markets are piled with all things succulent and toothsome, where the dinners of

Lucullus are eaten every day, and, if it be but cool, the very little greyhounds wear dainty little blankets—in these centres of wealth and power and refinement, there are always hungry men and women and little children. Never the sun goes down but on human beings prowling like wolves for food, or huddling together like vermin for shelter and warmth. "Always with You" is the significant heading under which a New York paper, in these most prosperous times, publishes daily the tales of chronic famine; and in the greatest and richest city of the world—in that very London, where the plenty of meat in the butchers' shops seemed to some savages the most wondrous of all its wonderful sights—in that very London, the mortuary reports have a standing column for deaths by starvation.

But no more in its chronic than in its spasmodic forms is famine to be measured by the deaths from starvation. Perfect, indeed, in all its parts must be the human machine if it can run till the last bit of available tissue be drawn on to feed its fires. It is under the guise of disease to which physicians can give less shocking names, that famine, especially the chronic famine of civilization, kills. And the statistics of mortality, especially of infant mortality, show that in the richest communities famine is constantly at its work. Insufficient nourishment, inadequate warmth and clothing, and unwholesome surroundings, constantly, in the very centres of plenty, swell the death rates. What is this but famine—just such famine as the Irish famine? It is not that the needed things are really scarce; but that those whose need is direst have not the means to get them, and, when not relieved by charity, want kills them in its various ways. When, in the hot midsummer, little children die like flies in the New York tenement wards, what is that but famine? And those barges crowded with such children that a noble and tender charity sends down New York harbour to catch the fresh salt breath of the Atlantic —are they not fighting famine as truly as was our food-laden war-ship and the Royal Prince's gunboats? Alas! to find famine one has not to cross the sea.

There was bitter satire in the cartoon that one of our illustrated papers published when subscriptions to the Irish famine fund were being made—a cartoon that represented James Gordon Bennett sailing away for Ireland in a boat loaded down with provisions, while a sad-eyed, hungry-looking, tattered group gazed wistfully on them from the pier. The bite and the bitterness of it, the humiliating sting and satire of it, were in its truth.

This is "the home of freedom," and "the asylum of the

oppressed;" our population is yet sparse, our public domain yet wide; we are the greatest of food producers, yet even here there are beggars, tramps, paupers, men torn by anxiety for the support of their families, women who know not which way to turn, little children growing up in such poverty and squalor that only a miracle can keep them pure. "Always with you," even here. What is the week or the day of the week that our papers do not tell of man or woman who, to escape the tortures of want, has stepped out of life unbidden? What is this but famine?

III.

Let me be understood. I am not endeavouring to excuse or belittle Irish distress. I am merely pointing out that distress of the same kind exists elsewhere. This is a fact I want to make clear, for it has hitherto, in most of the discussions of the Irish Land Question, been ignored. And without an appreciation of this fact the real nature of the Irish Land Question is not understood, nor the real importance of the agitation seen.

What I contend for is this: That it is a mistake to consider the Irish Land Question as a mere local question, arising out of conditions peculiar to Ireland, and which can be settled by remedies that can have but local application. On the contrary, I contend that what has been brought into prominence by Irish distress, and forced into discussion by Irish agitation, is something infinitely more important than any mere local question could be; it is nothing less than that question of transcendent importance which is everywhere beginning to agitate, and, if not settled, must soon convulse, the civilized world—the question whether, their political equality conceded (for, where this has not already been, it soon will be), the masses of mankind are to remain mere hewers of wood and drawers of water for the benefit of a fortunate few? whether, having escaped from feudalism, modern society is to pass into an industrial organisation more grinding and oppressive, more heartless and hopeless, than feudalism? whether, amid the abundance their labour creates, the producers of wealth are to be content in good times with the barest of livings, and in bad times to suffer and to starve? What is involved in this Irish Land Question is not a mere local matter between Irish landlords and Irish tenants, but the great social problem of modern civilization. What is arraigned in the arraignment of the claims of Irish landlords is nothing less than the widespread institution of private property in land. In the assertion of the natural rights of the Irish people is the assertion of the natural rights that, by virtue of his existence, pertain everywhere to man.

It is probable that the Irish agitators did not at first perceive the real bearing and importance of the question they took in hand. But they—the more intelligent and earnest of them, at least—must now begin to realise it.* Yet, save, perhaps, on the part of the ultra Tories, who would resist any concession as the opening of a door that can not again be shut, there is on all sides a disposition to ignore the real nature of the question, and to treat it as springing from conditions peculiar to Ireland. On the one hand, there is a large class in England and elsewhere, who, while willing to concede or even actually desiring that something should be done for Ireland, fear any extension of the agitation into a questioning of the rights of landowners elsewhere. And, on the other hand, the Irish leaders seem anxious to confine attention in the same way, evidently fearing that, should the question assume a broader aspect, strong forces now with them might fall away and, perhaps to a large extent, become directly and strongly antagonistic.

But it is not possible to so confine the discussion; no more possible than it was possible to confine to France the questions involved in the French Revolution; no more possible than it was possible to keep the discussion which arose over slavery in the Territories confined to the subject of slavery in the Territories. And it is best that the truth be fully stated and clearly recognised. He who sees the truth, let him proclaim it, without asking who is for it or who is against it. This is not radicalism in the bad sense which so many attach to the word. This is conservatism in the true sense.

What gives to the Irish Land Question its supreme significance is that it brings into attention and discussion—nay, that it forces into attention and discussion, not a mere Irish question, but a question of world-wide importance.

What has brought the land question to the front in Ireland, what permits the relations between land and labour to be seen there with such distinctness—to be seen even by those who can not in other places perceive them—is certain special conditions. Ireland is a country of dense population, so that competition for the use of land is so sharp and high as to produce marked effects upon the distribution of wealth. It is

* The *Irish World* which, though published in New-York, has exerted a large influence upon the agitation on both sides of the Atlantic, does realise, and has from the first frankly declared, that the fight must be against landlordism *in toto* and everywhere.

mainly an agricultural country, so that production is concerned directly and unmistakably with the soil. Its industrial organisation is largely that simple one in which an employing capitalist does not stand between labourer and landowner, so that the connection between rent and wages is not obscured. Ireland, moreover, was never conquered by the Romans, nor, until comparatively recently, by any people who had felt in their legal system the effect of Roman domination. It is the European country in which primitive ideas as to land tenures have longest held their sway, and the circumstances of its conquest, its cruel misgovernment, and the differences of race and religion between the masses of the people and those among whom the land was parcelled, have tended to preserve old traditions, and to direct the strength of Irish feeling and the fervour of Irish imagination against a system which forces the descendant of the ancient possessors of the soil to pay tribute for it to the representative of a hated stranger. It is for these reasons that the connection between Irish distress and Irish landlordism is so easily seen and readily realised.

But does not the same relation exist between English pauperism and English landlordism—between American tramps and the American land system? Essentially the same land system as that of Ireland exists elsewhere, and, wherever it exists, distress of essentially the same kind is to be seen. And elsewhere, just as certainly as in Ireland, is the connection between the two that of cause and effect.

When the agent of the Irish landlord takes from the Irish cottier for rent his pigs, his poultry, or his potatoes, or the money that he gains by the sale of these things, it is clear enough that this rent comes from the earnings of labour, and diminishes what the labourer gets. But is not this in reality just as clear when a dozen middle-men stand between labourer and landlord? Is it not just as clear when, instead of being paid monthly or quarterly or yearly, rent is paid in a lumped sum called purchase money? Whence come the incomes which the owners of land in mining districts, in manufacturing districts, or in commercial districts, receive for the use of their land? Manifestly, they must come from the earnings of labour—there is no other source from which they can come. From what are the revenues of Trinity Church corporation drawn, if not from the earnings of labour? What is the source of the income of the Astors, if it is not the labour of labouring men, women, and children? When a man makes a fortune by the rise of real estate, as in New York and elsewhere many men have done within the past few months, what does it mean? It means that he may have fine clothes, costly food, a grand house luxuriously furnished, etc. Now, these things are not the spontaneous fruits of the soil; neither do they fall from heaven, nor are they cast up by the sea. They are products of labour—can only be produced by labour. And hence, if men who do not labour get them, it must necessarily be at the expense of those who do labour.

It may seem as if I were needlessly dwelling upon a truth apparent by mere statement. Yet, simple as this truth is, it is persistently ignored. This is the reason that the true relation and true importance of the question which has come to the front in Ireland are so little realised.

To give an illustration: In his article in the "North American Review" last year, Mr Parnell speaks as though the building up of manufactures in Ireland would lessen the competition for land. What justification for such a view is there either in theory or in fact? Can manufacturing be carried on without land any more than agriculture can be carried on without land? Is not competition for land measured by price, and, if Ireland were a manufacturing country, would not the value of her land be greater than now? Had English clamour for "protection to home industry" not been suffered to secure the strangling of Irish industries in their infancy, Ireland might now be more of a manufacturing country with larger population and a greater aggregate production of wealth. But the tribute which the landowners could have taken would likewise have been greater. Put a Glasgow, a Manchester, or a London in one of the Irish agricultural counties, and, where the landlords now take pounds in rent, they would be enabled to demand hundreds and thousands of pounds. And it would necessarily come from the same source—the ultimate source of all incomes—the earnings of labour. That so large a proportion of the labouring class would not have to compete with each other for agricultural land is true. But they would have to do what is precisely the same thing. They would have to compete with each other for employment—for the opportunity to make a living. And there is no reason to think that this competition would be less intense than now. On the contrary, in the manufacturing districts of England and Scotland, just as in the agricultural districts of Ireland, the competition for the privilege of earning a living forces wages to such a minimum as, even in good times, will only give a living.

What is the difference? The Irish peasant cultivator hires his little farm from a landlord, and pays rent directly. The English agricultural labourer hires himself to an employing farmer who hires the land, and who out of the produce pays to the one his wages and to the other his rent. In both cases competition forces the labourer down to a bare living as a nett return for his work, and only stops at that point because, when men do not get enough to live on, they die and cease to compete. And, in the same way, competition forces the employing farmer to give up to the landlord all that he has left after paying wages, save the ordinary returns of capital—for the profits of the English farmer do not, on the average, I understand, exceed five or six per cent. And in other businesses, such as manufacturing, competition in the same way forces down wages to the minimum of a bare living, while rent goes up and up. Thus is it clear that no change in methods or improvements in the processes of industry lessens the landlord's power of claiming the lion's share.

I am utterly unable to see in what essential thing the condition of the Irish peasant would be a whit improved were Ireland as rich as England, and her industries as diversified. For the Irish peasant is not to be compared with the English tenant-farmer, who is really a capitalist, but with the English agricultural labourer and the lowest class of factory operatives. Surely their condition is not so much better than that of the Irish peasant as to make a difference worth talking about. On the contrary, miserable as is the condition of the Irish peasantry, sickening as are the stories of their suffering, I am inclined to think that for the worst instances of human degradation one must go to the reports that describe the condition of the labouring poor of England, rather than to the literature of Irish misery. For there are three things for which, in spite of their poverty and wretchedness and occasional famine, the very poorest of Irish peasants are by all accounts remarkable—the physical vigour of their men, the purity of their women, and the strength of the family affections. This, to put it mildly, can not be said of large classes of the labouring populations of England and Scotland. In those rich manufacturing districts are classes stunted and deteriorated physically by want and unwholesome employments; classes in which the idea of female virtue is all but lost, and the family affections all but trodden out.

But it is needless to compare sufferings and measure miseries. I merely wish to correct that impression which leads so many people to talk and write as though rent and land tenures related solely to agriculture and to agricultural communities. Nothing could be more erroneous, Land is necessary to all production, no matter what be its kind or form; land is the standing-place, the workshop, the store-house of labour; it is to the human being the only means by which he can obtain access to the material universe or utilize its powers. Without land man cannot exist. To whom the ownership of land is given, to him is given the virtual ownership of the men who must live upon it. When this necessity is absolute, then does he necessarily become their absolute master. And just as this point is neared—that is to say, just as competition increases the demand for land—just in that degree does the power of taking a larger and larger share of the earnings of labour increase. It is this power that gives land its value; this is the power that enables the owner of valuable land to reap where he has not sown—to appropriate to himself wealth which he has had no share in producing. Rent is always the devourer of wages. The owner of city land takes in the rents he receives for his land the earnings of labour just as clearly as does the owner of farming land. And whether he be working in a garret, ten stories above the street, or in a mining drift thousands of feet below the earth's surface, it is the competition for the use of land that ultimately determines what proportion of the produce of his labour the labourer will get for himself. This is the reason why modern progress does not tend to extirpate poverty; this is the reason why, with all the inventions and improvements and economies which so enormously increase productive power, wages everywhere tend to the minimum of a bare living. The cause that in Ireland produces poverty and distress—the ownership by some of the people of the land on which and from which the whole people must live—everywhere else produces the same results. It is this that produces the hideous squalor of London and Glasgow slums; it is this that makes want jostle luxury in the streets of rich New-York, that forces little children to monotonous and stunting toil in Massachusetts mills, and that fills the highways of our newest States with tramps.

IV.

The facts we have been considering give to the Irish agitation a significance and dignity that no effort for the redress of merely local grievances, no struggle for mere national independence, could have. As the cause which produces Irish distress exists everywhere throughout modern civilization, and everywhere produces the same results, the question as to what measures will fully meet the case of Ireland has for us not merely a speculative and sentimental interest, but a direct and personal interest.

For a year and more the English journals and magazines have been teeming with articles on the Irish Land Question; but, among all the remedies proposed even by men whose reputation is that of clear thinkers and advanced Liberals, I have seen nothing which shows any adequate grasp of the subject. And this is true also of the measures proposed by the agitators, so far as they have proposed any. They are illogical and insufficient to the last degree. They neither disclose any clear principle nor do they aim at any result worth the struggle.

From the most timid to the most radical, these schemes embrace one or more of the following propositions:—

1st, To abolish entails and primogenitures and other legal difficulties in the way of sales.

2nd, To legalise and extend tenant-right.

3rd, To establish tribunals of arbitrament which shall decide upon appeal as to the rent to be paid.

4th, To have the State buy out the landlords and sell again on time to the tenants.

The first of these propositions is good in itself. To make the transfer of land easy would be to remove obstacles which prevent its passing into the hands of those who would make the most out of it. But, so far as this will have any effect at all, it will not be toward giving the Irish tenants more merciful landlords; nor yet will it be to the diffusion of landed property. Those who think so shut their eyes to the fact that the tendency of the time is to concentration.

As for the propositions which look in various forms to the establishment of tenant-right, it is to be observed that, in so far as they go beyond giving the tenant surety for his improvements, they merely carve out of the estate of the landlord an estate for the tenant. Even if the proposal to empower the courts, in cases of dispute, to decide what is a fair rent were to amount to anything (and the Land Leaguers say it would not), the fixing of a lower rent as the share of the landlord would merely enable the tenant to charge a higher price to his successor. Whatever might thus be done for present agricultural tenants would be of no use to future tenants, and nothing whatever would be done for the masses of the people. In fact, that the effect would be to increase rent in the aggregate, there can be no doubt. Whatever modification might be made in the landlord's demands, the sum which the outgoing tenant would ask would be very certain to be all he could possibly get, so that rent in the aggregate, instead of being diminished, would be screwed up to the full competition or rack-rent standard.

What seem to be considered the most radical propositions yet made are those for the creation of a "peasant proprietary"—the State to buy out the landlords and resell to the tenants, for annual payments extending over a term of years, and covering principal and interest. Waiving all practical difficulties, and they are very great, what could thus be accomplished? Nothing real and permanent. For not merely is this, too, but a partial measure, which could not improve the condition of the masses of the people, or help those most needing help, but no sooner were the lands thus divided than a process of concentration would infallibly set in, which would be all the more rapid from the fact that the new landholders would be heavily mortgaged. The tendency to concentration, which has so steadily operated in Great Britain, and is so plainly showing itself in our new States, must operate in Ireland, and would immediately begin to weld together again the little patches of the newly created peasant proprietors. The tendency of the time is against peasant proprietorships; it is in everything to concentration, not to separation. The tendency which has wiped out the small landowners, the boasted yeomanry of England—which in our new States is uniting the quarter-sections of preemption and homestead settlers into great farms of thousands of acres—is already too strong to be resisted, and is constantly becoming stronger and more penetrating. For it springs from the inventions and improvements and economies which are transforming modern industry—the same influences which are concentrating population in large cities, business into the hands of great houses, and, for the blacksmith making his own nails, or the weaver working his own loom, substitutes the factory of the great corporation.

That a very great deal that the English advocates of peasant proprietorship have to say about the results of their favourite system in continental Europe is not borne out by the facts, any one who chooses to look over the testimony may see. But it is useless to discuss that. Peasant proprietorship in continental Europe is a survival, It exists only among populations which have not felt fully the breath of the new era. It continues to exist only by virtue of conditions which do not obtain in Ireland. The Irish peasant is not the French or Belgian peasant. He is in the habit of having very "long families," they very short ones. He has become familiar with the idea of emigrating; they have not. He can hardly be expected to have acquired those habits of close economy and careful forethought for which they are so remarkable; and there are various agencies, among which are to be counted the national schools and the present agitation, that have roused in him aspirations and ambitions which would prevent him from continuing to water his little patch with his sweat, as do the French and Belgian peasant proprietors, when he could sell it for enough to emigrate. Peasant proprietorship, like that of France and Belgium, might possibly have been instituted in Ireland some time ago, before the railroad and the telegraph and the national schools and the establishment of the steam bridge across the Atlantic. But to do it now to any extent, and with any permanency, seems to me about as practicable as to go back to hand-loom weaving in Manchester. Much more in accordance with modern tendencies is the notice I have recently seen of the formation of a company to buy up land in southern Ireland, and cultivate it on a large scale; for to production on a large scale modern processes more and more strongly tend. It is not merely the steam-plough and harvesting machinery that make the cultivation of the large field more profitable than that of the small one; it is the railroad, the telegraph, the manifold inventions of all sorts. Even butter and cheese are now made and chickens hatched and fattened in factories.

But the fatal defect of all these schemes as remedial measures is, that they do not go to the cause of the disease. What they propose to do, they propose to do merely for one class of the Irish people—the agricultural tenants. Now, the agricultural tenants are not so large nor so poor a class (among them are in fact many large capitalist farmers of the English type) as the agricultural labourers, while besides these there are the labourers of other kinds—the artisans, operatives, and poorer classes of the cities. What extension of tenant-right or conversion of tenants into partial or absolute proprietors is to benefit them? Even if the number of owners of Irish soil could thus be increased, the soil of Ireland would still be in the hands of a class, though of a somewhat larger class. And the spring of Irish misery would be untouched. Those who had merely their labour would be as badly off as now, if not in some respects worse off. Rent would still devour wages, and the injustice involved in the present system would be intrenched by the increase in the number who seemingly profit by it.

It is that peasant proprietors would strengthen the existing system that makes schemes for creating them so popular among certain sections of the propertied classes of Great Britain. This is the ground on which these schemes are largely urged. These small landowners are desired that they may be used as a buffer and bulwark against any questioning of the claims of the larger owners. They would be put forward to resist the shock of "agrarianism," just as the women are put forward in resistance to the process servers. "What! do you propose to rob these poor peasants of their little homesteads?" would be the answer to any one who proposed to attack the system under which the larger landholders draw millions annually from the produce of labour.

And here is the danger in the adoption of measures not based upon correct principles. They not only fail to do any real and permanent good, but they make proper measures more difficult. Even if a majority of the people of Ireland were made owners of the soil, the injustice to the minority would be as great as now, and wages would still tend to the minimum, which in good times means a bare living, and in bad times means starvation. Even were it possible to cut up the soil of Ireland into those little patches into which the soil of France and Belgium is cut in the districts where the *morcellement* prevails, this would not be the attainment of a just and healthy social state. But it would make the attainment of a just and healthy social state much more difficult.

V.

What, then, is the true solution of the Irish problem? The answer is as important to other countries as to Ireland, for the Irish problem is but a local phase of the great problem which is everywhere pressing upon the civilized world.

With the leaders of the Irish movement, the question is, of course, not merely what ought to be done, but what can be done. But, to a clear understanding of the whole subject, the question of principle must necessarily precede that of method. We must decide where we want to go before we can decide what is the best road to take.

The first question that naturally arises is that of right. Among whatever kind of people such a matter as this is discussed, the question of right is sure to be raised. This, to me, seems a very significant thing; for I believe it to spring from nothing less than a universal perception of the human mind—a perception often dim and vague, yet still a universal perception, that justice is the supreme law of the universe, so that, as a short road to what is best, we instinctively ask what is right?

Now, what are the rights of this case? To whom rightfully does the soil of Ireland belong? Who are justly entitled to its use and to all the benefits that flow from its use? Let us settle this question clearly and decisively, before we attempt anything else.

Let me go to the heart of this question by asking another question: Has or has not the child born in Ireland a right to live? There can be but one answer, for no one would contend that it was right to drown Irish babies, or that any human law could make it right. Well, then, if every human being born in Ireland has a right to live in Ireland, these rights must be equal. If each one has a right to live, then no one can have any better right to live than any other one. There can be no dispute about this. No one will contend that it would be any less a crime to drown the baby of an Irish peasant woman than it would be to drown the baby of the proudest duchess, or that a law commanding the one would be any more justifiable than a law commanding the other.

Since, then, all the Irish people have the same equal right to life, it follows that they must all have the same equal right to the land of Ireland. If they are all in Ireland by the same equal permission of Nature, so that no one of them can justly set up a superior claim to life than any other one of them; so that all the rest of them could not justly say to any one of them, "You have not the same right to live as we have; therefore we will pitch you out of Ireland into the sea!" then they must all have the same equal rights to the elements which Nature has provided for the sustaining of life—to air, to water, and to land. For to deny the equal right to the elements necessary to the maintaining of life is to deny the equal right to life. Any law that said, "Certain babies have no right to the soil of Ireland; therefore they shall be thrown off the soil of Ireland," would be precisely equivalent to a law that said, "Certain babies have no right to live; therefore they shall be thrown into the sea." And as no law or custom or agreement can justify the denial of the equal right to life, so no law or custom or agreement can justify the denial of the equal right to land.

It therefore follows, from the very fact of their existence, that the right of each one of the people of Ireland to an equal share in the land of Ireland is equal and inalienable: that is to say, that the use and benefit of the land of Ireland belong rightfully to the whole people of Ireland, to each one as much as to every other; to no one more than to any other—not to some individuals, to the exclusion of other individuals; not to one class, to the exclusion of other classes; not to landlords, not to tenants, not to cultivators, but to the whole people.

This right is irrefutable and indefeasible. It pertains to

and springs from the fact of existence, the right to live. No law, no covenant, no agreement, can bar it. One generation cannot stipulate away the rights of another generation. If the whole people of Ireland were to unite in bargaining away their rights in the land, how could they justly bargain away the right of the child who the next moment is born? No one can bargain away what is not his; no one can stipulate away the rights of another. And if the new-born infant has an equal right to life, then has it an equal right to land. Its warrant, which comes direct from Nature, and which sets aside all human laws or title-deeds, is the fact that it is born.

Here we have a firm, self-apparent principle from which we may safely proceed. The land of Ireland does not belong to one individual more than to another individual, to one class more than to another class; to one generation more than to the generations that come after. It belongs to the whole people who at the time exist upon it.

VI.

I do not dwell upon this principle because it has not yet been asserted. I dwell upon it because, although it has been asserted, no proposal to carry it out has yet been made. The cry has indeed gone up that the land of Ireland belongs to the people of Ireland, but there the recognition of the principle has stopped. To say that the land of Ireland belongs to the people of Ireland, and then merely to ask that rents shall be reduced, or that tenant-right be extended, or that the State shall buy the land from one class and sell it to another class, is utterly illogical and absurd.

Either the land of Ireland rightfully belongs to the Irish landlords, or it rightfully belongs to the Irish people; there can be no middle ground. If it rightfully belongs to the landlords, then is the whole agitation wrong, and every scheme for interfering in any way with the landlords is condemned. If the land rightfully belongs to the landlords, then it is nobody else's business what they do with it, or what rent they charge for it, or where or how they spend the money they draw from it, and whoever does not want to live upon it on the landlord's terms is at perfect liberty to starve or emigrate. But if, on the contrary, the land of Ireland rightfully belongs to the Irish people, then the only logical demand is, not that the tenants shall be made joint owners with the landlords—not that it be bought from a smaller class and sold to a larger class, but that it be resumed by the whole people To propose to pay the landlords for it, is to deny the right of the people to it. The real fight for Irish rights must be made outside of Ireland; and, above all things, the Irish agitators ought to take a logical position, based upon a broad, clear principle, which can be everywhere understood and appreciated. To ask for tenant-right or peasant proprietorship is not to take such a position; to concede that the landlords ought to be paid is to utterly abandon the principle that the land rightfully belongs to the people.

To admit, as even the most radical of the Irish agitators seem to admit, that the landlords should be paid the full value of their lands, is to deny the rights of the people. It is an admission that the agitation is an interference with the just rights of property. It is to ignore the only principle on which the agitation can be justified, and on which it can gather strength for the accomplishment of anything real and permanent. To admit this is to admit that the Irish people have no more right to the soil of Ireland than any outsider; for any outsider can go to Ireland and buy land, if he will give its market value. To propose to buy out the landlords is to propose to continue the present injustice in another form. They would get in interest on the debt created what they now get in rent. They would still have a lien upon Irish labour.

And why should the landlords be paid? If the land of Ireland belongs of natural right to the Irish people, what valid claim for payment can be set up by the Irish landlords? No one will contend that the land is theirs of natural right, for the day has gone by when men could be told that the Creator of the universe intended his bounty for the exclusive use and benefit of a privileged class of his creatures—that he intended a few to roll in luxury, while their fellows toiled and starved for them. The claim of the landlords to the land rests not on natural right, but merely on municipal law—on municipal law which contravenes natural right. And, whenever the sovereign power changes municipal law so as to conform to natural right, what claim can they assert to compensation? Some of them bought their lands, it is true; but they got no better title than the seller had to give. And what are these titles? Titles based on murder and robbery, on blood and rapine—titles which rest on the most atrocious and wholesale crimes. Created by force and maintained by force, they have not behind them the first shadow of right. That Henry II. and James I. and Cromwell and the Long Parliament had the power to give and grant Irish lands is true? But will any one contend they had the right? Will any one contend that in all the past generations there has existed on the British Isles, or anywhere else, any human being, or any number of human beings, who had the right to say that in the year 1881 the great mass of Irishmen should be compelled to pay—in many cases to residents of England, France, or the United States—for the privilege of living in their native country and making a living from their native soil? Even if it be said that might makes right; even if it be contended that in the twelfth, or seventeenth, or eighteenth century lived men who, having the power, had therefore the right, to give away the soil of Ireland, it will not be contended that their right went further than their power, or that their gifts and grants are binding on the men of the present generation. No one can urge such a preposterous doctrine. And, if might makes right, then the moment the people get power to take the land the rights of the present landholders utterly cease, and any proposal to compensate them is a proposal to do a fresh wrong.

Should it be urged that, no matter on what they originally rest, the lapse of time has given to the legal owners of Irish land a title of which they cannot now be justly deprived without compensation, it is sufficient to ask, with Herbert Spencer, at what rate per annum wrong becomes right? Even the shallow pretence that the acquiescence of society can vest in a few the exclusive right to that element on which and from which Nature has ordained that all must live, cannot be urged in the case of Ireland. For the Irish people have never acquiesced in their spoliation, unless the bound and gagged victim may be said to acquiesce in the robbery and maltreatment which he cannot prevent. Though the memory of their ancient rights in the land of their country may have been utterly stamped out among the people of England, and have been utterly forgotten among their kin on this side of the sea, it has long survived among the Irish. If the Irish people have gone hungry and cold and ignorant, if they have been evicted from lands on which their ancestors had lived from time immemorial, if they have been forced to emigrate or to starve, it has not been for want of protest. They have protested all they could; they have struggled all they could. It has been but superior force that has stifled their protests and made their struggles vain. In a blind, dumb way, they are protesting now and struggling now, though even if their hands were free they might not at first know how to untie the knots in the cords that bind them. But acquiesce they never have.

Yet, even supposing they had acquiesced, as in their ignorance the working-classes of such countries as England and the United States now acquiesce, in the iniquitous system which makes the common birthright of all the exclusive property of some. What then? Does such acquiescence turn wrong into right? If the sleeping traveller wake to find a robber with his hand in his pocket, is he bound to buy the robber off—bound not merely to let him keep what he has previously taken, but pay him the full value of all he expected the sleep of his victim to permit him to get? If the stockholders of a bank find that for a long term of years their cashier has been appropriating the lion's share of the profits, are they to be told that they cannot discharge him without paying him for what he might have got, had his peculations not been discovered?

VII.

I apologise to the Irish landlords and to all other landlords for likening them to thieves and robbers. They will, however, understand that I do not consider them as personally worse than other men, but that I am obliged to use such illustrations because no others will fit the case. I am concerned not with individuals, but with the system. What I want to do is, to point out a distinction that in the plea for the vested rights of landowners is ignored—a distinction which arises from the essential difference between land and things which are the produce of human labour, and which is obscured by our habit of classing them all together as property.

The galleys that carried Cæsar to Britain, the accoutrements of his legionaries, the baggage that they carried, the arms that they bore, the buildings that they erected; the scythed chariots of the ancient Britons, the horses that drew them, their wicker boats and wattled houses—where are they now? But the land for which Roman and Briton fought, there it is still. That British soil is yet as fresh and as new as it was in the days of the Romans. Generation after generation has lived on it since, and generation after generation will live on it yet. Now, here is a very great difference. The right to possess and to pass on the ownership of things that in their nature decay and soon cease to be is a very different thing from the right to possess and to pass on the ownership of that which does not decay, but from which each successive generation must live.

To show how this difference between land and such other species of property as are properly styled wealth bears upon the argument for the vested rights of landowners, let me illustrate again.

Captain Kidd was a pirate. He made a business of sailing the seas, capturing merchantmen, making their crews walk the plank, and appropriating their cargoes. In this way he accumulated much wealth, which he is thought to have buried But let us suppose, for the sake of the illustration, that he did not bury his wealth, but left it to his legal heirs, and they to their heirs, and so on, until at the present day this wealth or a part of it has come to a great-great-grandson of Captain Kidd. Now, let us suppose that some one—say a great-great-grandson of one of the ship-masters whom Captain Kidd plundered, makes complaint and says: "This man's great-great-grandfather plundered my great-great-grandfather of certain things or certain sums which have been transmitted to him, whereas but for this wrongful act they would have been transmitted to me; therefore I demand that he be made to restore them." What would society answer?

Society, speaking by its proper tribunals, and in accordance with principles recognised among all civilised nations, would say: "We cannot entertain such a demand. It may be true that Mr. Kidd's great-great-grandfather robbed your great-great-grandfather, and that as the result of this wrong he has got things that otherwise might have come to you. But we cannot inquire into occurrences that happened so long ago. Each generation has enough to do to attend to its own affairs. If we go to righting the wrongs and reopening the controversies of our great-great-grandfathers, there would be no end to disputes and pretexts for disputes. What you say may be true, but somewhere we must draw the line, and have an end to strife. Though this man's great-great-grandfather may have robbed your great-great-grandfather, *he* has not robbed *you*. He came into possession of these things peacefully, and has held them peacefully, and we must take this peaceful possession, when it has been continued for a certain time, as absolute evidence of just title; for, were we not to do that, there would be no end to dispute and no secure possession of anything."

Now, it is this common-sense principle that is expressed in the statute of limitations—in the doctrine of vested rights. This is the reason why it is held—and as to most things held justly—that peaceable possession for a certain time cures all defects of title.

But let us pursue the illustration a little further:

Let us suppose that Captain Kidd, having established a large and profitable piratical business, left it to his son, and he to his son, and so on, until his great-great-grandson, who now pursues it, has come to consider it the most natural thing in the world that his ships should roam the sea, capturing peaceful merchantmen, making their crews walk the plank, and bringing home to him much plunder, whereby he is enabled, though he does no work at all, to live in very great luxury, and look down with contempt upon people who have to work. But at last, let us suppose, the merchants get tired of having their ships sunk and their goods taken, and sailors get tired of trembling for their lives every time a sail lifts above the horizon, and they demand of society that piracy be stopped.

Now, what should society say if Mr. Kidd got indignant, appealed to the doctrine of vested rights, and asserted that society was bound to prevent any interference with the business that he had inherited, and that, if it wanted him to stop, it must buy him out, paying him all that his business was worth—that is to say, at least as much as he could make in twenty years' successful pirating, so that if he stopped pirating, he could still continue to live in luxury off the profits of the merchants, and the earnings of the sailors?

What ought society to say to such a claim as this. There will be but one answer. We will say that society should tell Mr. Kidd that his was a business to which the statute of limitations and the doctrine of vested rights did not apply; that because his father, and his grandfather, and his great and great-great-grandfather pursued the business of capturing ships and making their crews walk the plank, was no reason why he should be permitted to pursue it. Society, we will all agree, ought to say he would have to stop piracy, and stop it at once, and that without getting a cent for stopping.

Or supposing it had happened that Mr. Kidd had sold out his piratical business to Smith, Jones, or Robinson, we will all agree that society ought to say that their purchase of the business gave them no greater right than Mr. Kidd had.

We will all agree that that is what society *ought* to say. Observe, I do not ask what society *would* say.

For, ridiculous and preposterous as it may appear, I am satisfied that under the circumstances I have supposed, society would not for a long time say what we have agreed it *ought* to say. Not only would all the Kidds loudly claim that to make them give up their business without full recompense would be a wicked interference with vested rights, but the justice of this claim would at first be assumed as a matter of course by all or nearly all the influential classes—the great lawyers, the able journalists, the writers for the magazines, the eloquent clergymen, and the principal professors in the principal universities. Nay, even the merchants and sailors, when they first began to complain, would be so tyrannised and browbeaten by this public opinion, that they would hardly think of more than of buying out the Kidds, and, wherever here and there any one dared to raise his voice in favour of stopping piracy at once and without compensation, he would only do so under penalty of being stigmatised as a reckless disturber and wicked foe of social order.

If any one denies this, if any one says mankind are not such fools, then I appeal to universal history to bear me witness. I appeal to the facts of to-day.

Show me a wrong, no matter how monstrous, that ever yet among any people became ingrafted in the social system, and I will prove to you the truth of what I say.

The majority of men do not think; the majority of men have to expend so much energy in the struggle to make a living that they do not have time to think. The majority of men accept, as a matter of course, whatever is. This is what makes the task of the social reformer so difficult, his path so hard. This is what brings to those who first raise their voices in behalf of a great truth the sneers of the powerful, and the curses of the rabble, ostracism and martyrdom, the robe of derision and the crown of thorns.

Am I not right? Have there not been states of society in which piracy has been considered the most respectable and honourable of pursuits? Did the Roman populace see anything more reprehensible in a gladiatorial show than we do in a horse-race? Does public opinion in Dahomey see anything reprehensible in the custom of sacrificing a thousand or two human beings by way of signalising grand occasions? Are there not states of society in which, in spite of the natural proportions of the sexes, polygamy is considered a matter of course? Are there not states of society in which it would be considered the most ridiculous thing in the world, to say that a man's son was more closely related to him than his nephew? Are there not states of society in which it would be considered disreputable for a man to carry a burden, while a woman who could stagger under it was around?—states of society in which the husband, who did not occasionally beat his wife, would be deemed by both sexes a weak-minded, low-spirited fellow? What would Chinese fashionable society consider more outrageous than to be told that mothers should not be permitted to squeeze their daughters' feet, or Flathead women than being restrained from tying a board on their infants' skulls? How long has it been since the monstrous doctrine of the divine right of kings was taught through all Christendom?

What is the slave trade but piracy of the worst kind? Yet it is not long since the slave trade was looked upon as a perfectly respectable business, affording as legitimate an opening for the investment of capital and the display of enterprise as any other. The proposition to prohibit it was first looked upon as ridiculous, then as fanatical, then as wicked. It was only slowly and by hard fighting that the truth in regard to it gained ground. Does not our very Constitution bear witness to what I say? Does not the fundamental law of the nation, adopted twelve years after the annunciation of the Declaration of Independence, declare that for twenty years the slave trade shall not be prohibited nor restricted? Such dominion had the idea of vested interests over the minds of those who had already proclaimed the inalienable right of man to life, liberty, and the pursuit of happiness!

Is it not but yesterday that in the freest and greatest republic on earth, among the people who boast that they lead the very van of civilization, this doctrine of vested rights was deemed a sufficient justification for all the cruel wrongs of human slavery? Is it not but yesterday, when whoever dared to say that the rights of property did not justly attach to human beings; when whoever dared to deny that human beings could not be rightfully bought and sold like cattle—the husband torn from the wife and the child from the mother; when whoever denied the right of whoever had paid his money for him to work or whip his own nigger was looked upon as a wicked assailant of the rights of property? Is it not but yesterday when in the South whoever whispered such a thought took his life in his hands; when in the North the abolitionist was held by the churches as worse than an infidel, was denounced by the politicians and rotten-egged by the mob? I was born in a Northern State, I have never lived in the South, I am not yet grey; but I well remember, as every American of middle age must remember, how over and over again I have heard all questionings of slavery silenced by the declaration that the negroes were the *property* of their masters, and that to take away a man's slave without payment was as much a crime as to take away his horse without payment. And whoever does not remember that far back, let him look over American literature previous to the war, and say whether, if the business of piracy had been a flourishing business, it would have lacked defenders? Let him say whether any proposal to stop the business of piracy without compensating the pirates would not have been denounced at first as a proposal to set aside vested rights?

But I am appealing to other states of society and to times that are past merely to get my readers, if I can, out of their accustomed ruts of thought. The proof of what I assert about the Kidds and their business is in the thought and speech of to-day.

Here is a system which robs the producers of wealth as remorselessly and far more regularly and systematically than the pirate robs the merchantman. Here is a system that steadily condemns thousands to far more lingering and horrible deaths than walking the plank—to death of the mind and death of the soul, as well as death of the body. These things are undisputed. No one denies that Irish pauperism and famine are the direct results of this land system, and no one who will examine the subject will deny that the chronic pauperism and chronic famine which everywhere mark our civilization are the results of this system. Yet we are told—nay, it seems to be taken for granted—that this system can not be abolished without buying off those who profit by it. Was there ever more degrading abasement of the human mind before a fetish? Can we wonder, as we see it, at any perversion of ideas?

Consider: is not the parallel I have drawn a true one? Is it not just as much a perversion of ideas to apply the doctrine of vested rights to property in land, when these are its admitted fruits, as it was to apply it to property in human flesh and blood; as it would be to apply it to the business of piracy? In what does the claim of the Irish landholders differ from that of the hereditary pirate or the man who has bought out a piratical business? "Because I have inherited or purchased the business of robbing merchantmen," says the pirate, "therefore respect for the rights of property must compel you to let me go on robbing ships and making sailors walk the plank until you buy me out." "Because we have inherited or purchased the privilege of appropriating to ourselves the lion's share of the produce of labour," says the landlord, "therefore you must continue to let us do it, even though poor wretches shiver with cold and faint with hunger, even though, in their poverty and misery, they are reduced to wallow with the pigs." What is the difference?

This is the point I want to make clearly and distinctly, for it shows a distinction that in current thought is overlooked. Property in land, like property in slaves, is essentially different from property in things that are the result of labour. Rob a man or a people of money, or goods, or cattle, and the robbery is finished there and then. The lapse of time does not, indeed, change wrong into right, but it obliterates the effects of the deed. That is done; it is over; and, unless it be very soon righted, it glides away into the past, with the men who were parties to it, so swiftly that nothing save omniscience can trace its effects; and in attempting to right it we would be in danger of doing fresh wrong. The past is forever beyond us. We can neither punish nor recompense the dead. But rob a people of the land on which they must live, and the robbery is continuous. It is a fresh robbery of every succeeding generation—a new robbery every year and every day; it is like the robbery which condemns to slavery the children of the slave. To apply to it the statute of limitations, to acknowledge for it the title of prescription, is not to condone the past; it is to legalise robbery in the present, to justify it in the future. The indictment which really lies against the Irish landlords is not that their ancestors, or the ancestors of their grantors, robbed the ancestors of the Irish people. That makes no difference. "Let the dead bury their dead." The indictment that truly lies is that here, now, in the year 1881, *they* robbed the Irish people. And shall we be told that there can be a vested right to continue such robbery?

VIII.

I have dwelt so long upon this question of compensating landowners, not merely because it is of great practical importance, but because its discussion brings clearly into view the principles upon which the land question in Ireland, or in any other country, can alone be justly and finally settled. In the light of these principles we see that the landowners have no rightful claim either to the land or to compensation for its resumption by the people, and, further than that, we see that no such rightful claim can ever be created. It would be wrong to pay the present landowners for "their" land at the expense of the people; it would likewise be wrong to sell it again to smaller holders. It would be wrong to abolish the payment of rent, and to give the land to its present cultivators. In the very nature of things, land can not rightfully be made individual property. This principle is absolute. The title of a peasant proprietor deserves no more respect than the title of a great territorial noble. Neither the sovereign power of Great Britain, nor the whole people of Ireland, nor the whole population of the globe, can give to an individual a valid title to a square inch of Irish soil or any other soil. The earth is an entailed estate—entailed upon all the generations of the children of men, by a deed written in the constitution of Nature, a deed that no human proceedings can bar, and no prescription determine. Each succeeding generation has but a tenancy for life. Admitting that any set of men may barter away their own natural rights (and this logically involves an admission of the right of suicide), they can no more barter away the rights of their successors than they can barter away the rights of the inhabitants of other worlds.

What should be aimed at in the settlement of the Irish Land Question is thus very clear. The "three F's" are, what they have already been called, three frauds; and the proposition to create peasant proprietorship is no better. It will not do merely to carve out of the estates of the landlords a minor estate for the tenants; it will not do merely to substitute a larger for a smaller class of proprietors; it will not do to confine the settlement to agricultural land, leaving to its present possessors the land of the towns and villages. None of these lame and impotent propositions will satisfy the demands of justice or cure the bitter evils now so apparent. The only true and just solution of the problem, the only end worth aiming at, is to make *all* the land the common property of *all* the people.

This principle conceded, the question of method arises. How shall this be done? Nothing is easier. It is merely necessary to divert the rent which now flows into the pockets of the landlords into the common treasury of the whole people. It is not possible to so divide up the land of Ireland so as to give each family, still less each individual, an equal share. And, even if that were possible, it would not be possible to maintain equality, for old people are constantly dying and new people constantly being born. But it is possible to equally divide the rent or, what amounts to the same thing, to apply it to purposes of common benefit. This is the way, and this is the only way in which absolute justice can be done. This is the way, and this is the only way, in which the equal right of every man, woman, and child can be acknowledged and secured As Herbert Spencer says of it:*

> Such a doctrine is consistent with the highest state of civilization; may be carried out without involving a community of goods, and need cause no very serious revolution in existing arrangements. The change required would simply be a change of landlords. Separate ownership would merge into the joint-stock ownership of the public. Instead of being in the possession of individuals, the country would be held by the great corporate body—society. Instead of leasing his acres from an isolated proprietor, the farmer would lease them from the nation. Instead of paying his rent to the agent of Sir John or his Grace, he would pay it to an agent or deputy agent of the community. Stewards would be public officials instead of private ones, and tenancy the only land tenure. A state of things so ordered would be in perfect harmony

* "Social Statics," Chap. IX., sec. 8.

with the moral law. Under it, all men would be equally landlords; all men would be alike free to become tenants. . . . Clearly, therefore, on such a system, the earth might be enclosed, occupied, and cultivated, in entire subordination to the law of equal freedom.

Now, it is a very easy thing to thus keep away all private ownership of land, and convert all occupiers into tenants of the State, by appropriating rent. No complicated laws or cumbersome machinery is necessary. It is only necessary to tax land up to its full value. Do that, and without any talk about dispossessing landlords, without any use of the ugly word "confiscation," without any infringement of the just rights of property, the land would become virtually the people's, while the landlords would be left the absolute and unqualified possessors of—their deeds of title and conveyance! They could continue to call themselves landlords, if they wished to, just as that poor old Bourbon, the Comte de Chambord, continues to call himself King of France; but, as what, under this system, was paid by the tenant would be taken by the State, it is pretty clear that middle-men would not long survive, and that very soon the occupiers of land would come to be nominally the owners, though, in reality, they would be the tenants of the whole people.

How beautifully this simple method would satisfy every economic requirement; how, freeing labour and capital from the fetters that now oppress them (for all other taxes could be easily remitted), it would enormously increase the production of wealth; how it would make distribution conform to the law of justice, dry up the springs of want and misery, elevate society from its lowest stratum, and give all their fair share in the blessings of advancing civilization, can perhaps only be fully shown by such a detailed examination of the whole social problem as I have made in a book which I hope will be read by all the readers of this paper,* since in it I go over much ground and treat many subjects which cannot be even touched upon here. Nevertheless, any one can see that to tax land up to its full rental value would amount to precisely the same thing as to formally take possession of it, and then let it out to the highest bidders.

IX.

We have now seen the point that should be aimed at, and the method by which it is to be reached. There is another branch of the subject which practical men must consider: the political forces that may be marshalled; the political resistance

* "Progress and Poverty."

that must be overcome. It is one thing to work out such a problem in the closet—to demonstrate its proper solution to the satisfaction of a few intelligent readers. It is another thing to solve it in the field of action, where ignorance, prejudice, and powerful interests must be met.

It cannot be that the really earnest men in the Irish movement are satisfied with any programme yet put forth. But they are doubtless influenced by the fear that the avowal of radical views and aims would not merely intensify present opposition, but frighten away from their cause large numbers and important influences now with it. To say nothing of English conservatism, there is in Ireland a large class now supporting the movement who are morbidly afraid of anything which savours of "communism" or "socialism," while in the United States, whence much moral support and pecuniary aid have been derived, it is certain that many of those who are now loudest in their expressions of sympathy would slink away from a movement which avowed the intention of abolishing private property in land. A resolution, expressive of sympathy with the Irish people in their "struggle for the repeal of oppressive land laws" was, by a unanimous vote of the National House of Representatives, flung full in the face of the British lion. How many votes would that resolution have got had it involved a declaration of hostility to the institution of individual property in land?

I understand all this. Nevertheless, I am convinced that the Irish land movement would gain, not lose, were its earnest leaders, disdaining timid counsels, to boldly avow the principle that the land of Ireland belongs of right to the whole people of Ireland, and, without bothering about compensation to the landholders, to propose its resumption by the people in the simple way I have suggested. That, in doing this, they would lose strength and increase antagonism in some directions is true, but they would in other directions gain strength and allay antagonisms. And, while the loss would constantly tend to diminish, the gain would constantly tend to increase. They would, to use the phrase of Emerson, have "hitched their waggon to a star."

I admit, as will be urged by those who would hold back from such an avowal as I propose, that political progress must be by short steps rather than by great leaps; that those who would have the people follow them readily, and especially those who would enjoy present popularity and preferment, must not go too far in advance; and that to demand a little at first is often the surest way to obtain much at last.

So far as personal consideration is concerned, it is only to earnest men capable of feeling the inspiration of a great principle that I care to talk, or that I can hope to convince. To them I wish to point out that caution is not wisdom when it involves the ignoring of a great principle; that it is not every step that involves progression, but only such steps as are in the right line and make easier the next; that there are strong forces that wait but the raising of the true standard to rally on its side.

Let the time-servers, the demagogues, the compromisers, to whom nothing is right and nothing is wrong, but who are always seeking to find some half-way house between right and wrong—let them all go their ways. Any cause which can lay hold of a great truth is the stronger without them. If the earnest men among the Irish leaders abandon their present half-hearted illogical position, and take their stand frankly and firmly upon the principle that the youngest child of the poorest peasant has as good a right to tread the soil and breathe the air of Ireland as the eldest son of the proudest duke, they will have put their fight on the right line. Present defeat will but pave the way for future victory, and each step won makes easier the next. Their position will not only be logically defensible, but will prove the stronger the more it is discussed; for private property in land, which never rises from the natural perceptions of men, but springs historically from usurpation and robbery, is something so utterly absurd, so outrageously unjust, so clearly a waste of productive forces and a barrier to the most profitable use of natural opportunities, so thoroughly opposed to all sound maxims of public policy, so glaringly in the way of further progress, that it is only tolerated because the majority of men never think about it or hear it questioned. Once fairly arraign it, and it must be condemned; once call upon its advocates to exhibit its claims, and their cause is lost in advance. There is to-day no political economist of standing who dare hazard his reputation by defending it on economic grounds; there is to-day no thinker of eminence who either does not, like Herbert Spencer, openly declare the injustice of private property in land, or tacitly make the same admission. Once force the discussion on this line, and the Irish reformers will compel to their side the most active and powerful of the men who mould thought.

And they will not merely close up their own ranks, now in danger of being broken; they will "carry the war into Africa," and make possible the most powerful of political combinations.

It is already beginning to be perceived that the Irish movement, so far as it has yet gone, is merely in the interest of a class; that, so far as it has yet voiced any demand, it promises nothing to the labouring and artisan classes. Its opponents already see this opportunity for division, which, even without their efforts, must soon show itself, and which, now that the first impulse of the movement is over, will the more readily develop. To close up its ranks, and hold them firm, so that, even though they be forced to bend, they will not break and scatter, it must cease to be a movement looking merely to the benefit of the tenant-farmer, and become a movement for the benefit of the whole labouring class.

And the moment this is done the Irish land agitation assumes a new and a grander phase. It ceases to be an Irish movement; it becomes but the van of a world-wide struggle. Count the loss and the gain.

X.

The Land League movement, as an Irish movement, has in its favour the strength of Irish national feeling. In assuming the radical ground I urge, it would lose some of this; for their are doubtless a considerable number of Irishmen on both sides of the Atlantic who would shrink at first from the proposal to abolish private property in land. But all that is worth having would soon come back to it. And its strength would be more compact and intense—animated by a more definite purpose and a more profound conviction.

But in ceasing to be a movement having relation simply to Ireland—in proclaiming a truth and proposing a remedy which apply as well to every other country—it would allay opposition, which, as a mere national movement, it arouses, and bring to its support forces by which alone it can conquer.

England, not Ireland, is the field where the struggle for the natural rights of Irishmen must be won, if won at all. The powerful landed interest of England is against the movement anyhow. The natural allies of the Irish agitators are the English working classes—not merely the Irishmen and sons of Irishmen who, in the larger English cities, are numerous enough to make some show and exert some voting power, without being numerous enough to effect any important result—but the great labouring masses of Great Britain. So long as merely Irish measures are proposed, they cannot gain the hearty support even of the English radicals; so long as race prejudices and hatreds are appealed to, counter prejudices and hatreds must be aroused.

It is the very madness of folly, it is one of those political blunders worse than crimes, to permit in this land agitation that indiscriminating denunciation of England and everything English which is so common at Land League meetings and in the newspapers which voice Irish sentiment. The men who do this may be giving way to a natural sentiment; but they are most effectually doing the work of the real oppressors of Ireland. Were they secret emissaries of the London police, were they bribed with the gold which the British oligarchy grinds out of the toil of its white slaves in mill, and mine, and field, they could not better be doing its work. "Divide and conquer" is the golden maxim of the oppressors of mankind. It is by arousing race antipathies and exciting national animosities, by appealing to local prejudices and setting people against people, that aristocracies and despotisms have been founded and maintained. They who would free men must rise above such feelings if they would be successful. The greatest enemy of the people's cause is he who appeals to national passion and excites old hatreds. He is its best friend who does his utmost to bury them out of sight. For that action and reaction are equal and uniform is the law of the moral as of the physical world. Herein lies the far-reaching sweep of those sublime teachings that, after centuries of nominal acceptance, the so-called Christian world yet ignores, and which call on us to answer not revilings with revilings, but to meet hatred with love. "For," as say the Scriptures of the Buddhists, "hatred never ceases by hatred at any time; hatred ceases by love; that is an old rule." To denounce Englishmen is simply to arouse the prejudices and excite the animosities of Englishmen—to separate forces that ought to be united. To make this the fight of the Irish people against the English people is to doom it to failure. To make it the common cause of the people everywhere against a system which everywhere oppresses and robs them is to make its success assured. Had this been made to appear, the Irish members would not have stood alone when it came to the final resistance to coercion. Had this been made to appear, all England would be in a ferment at the proposal to give the Government despotic powers. If the Irish leaders are wise, they may yet avail themselves of the rising tide of English democracy. Let the Land Leaguers adopt the noble maxim of the German Social Democrats. Let them be Land Leaguers first, and Irishmen afterward. Let them account him an enemy of their cause who seeks to pander to prejudice and arouse hate. Let them arouse to a higher love than the mere love of country; to a wider patriotism than that which exhausts itself on one little subdivision of the human race, one little spot on the great earth's surface; and in this name, and by this sign, call upon their brothers, not merely to aid them, but to strike for themselves.

In so far as home rule means local self-government, in so far as it can be demanded for the benefit of all sections of the British empire, it is good; but talk of Irish independence is as harmful as it is wild and vain. The political separation of Ireland from England is impossible. And to both countries it could work but ill. The English people could no more consent to separation than we could consent to secession, and, if they did, it would be a step backward, not a step forward. All the tendencies of the time are not to separation, but to integration; not to independence, but to interdependence. This is observable wherever modern influences reach, and in all things. To attempt to resist it is to attempt to turn back the tide of progress.

It is not with the English people that the Irish people have cause of quarrel. It is with the system that oppresses both. That is the thing to denounce; that is the thing to fight. And it is to be fought most effectually by uniting the masses against it. Monarchy, aristocracy, landlordism, would get but a new lease of life by any attempt at separation which would arouse sectional passions. They are strengthened by any talk of it. The greatest blow that could be struck against them would be, scrupulously avoiding everything that could excite antagonistic national feeling, to carry this land agitation into England, not as a mere Irish question, but as an English question as well. To proclaim the universal truth that land is of natural right common property; to abandon all timid and half-way schemes which attempt to compromise between justice and injustice, and to demand nothing more nor less than a full recognition of this natural right would be to do this. It would inevitably be to put the English masses upon inquiry; to put English landholders upon the defensive, and give them more than enough to do at home. England is ripe for such an agitation, and, once fairly begun, it can have but one result—the victory of the popular cause.

XI.

Nor is it merely the labouring classes of England who may thus be brought into the fight, if the true standard be raised. To demand the nationalization of land by the simple means I have proposed makes possible—nay, as the discussion goes on, makes inevitable—an irresistible combination, the combination of labour and capital against landlordism. This combination proved its power by winning the battle of free trade in 1846 against the most determined resistance of the landed interest. It would be much more powerful now, and, if it can again be made on the land question, it can again force the entrenchments of the landed aristocracy.

Now, this combination cannot be made on any of the timid, illogical schemes as yet proposed; but it *can* be made on the broad principle that land is rightfully common property. Paradoxical as it may seem, it is yet true that, while the present position of the Irish agitators *does* involve a menace to capital, the absolute denial of the right of private property in land *would not*.

In admitting that the Irish landlords ought to get any rent at all, in admitting that, if the land is taken from them, they must be paid for it, the Irish agitators give away their whole case. For in this they admit that the land really belongs to the landlord, and put property in land in the same category with other property. Thus they place themselves in an indefensible position; thus they give to the agitation a "communistic"* character, and excite against it that natural and proper feeling which strongly resents any attack upon the rights of property as an attack upon the very foundations of society. It was doubtless this mistake of the agitators in admitting the right of private property in land to which Archbishop McCabe recently alluded in saying that some of the utterances of the agitators excited the solicitude of the Holy See. For this mistake gives to the agitation the character of an attack upon the rights of property. If the land is really the property of the landlords (and this is admitted when it is admitted that they are entitled to any rent or to any compensation), then to limit the rent which they shall get, or to interfere with their freedom to make what terms they please with tenants, is an attack upon property rights. If the land is rightfully the landlords', then is any compulsion as to how they shall let it, or on what terms they shall part with it, a bad and dangerous precedent, which naturally alarms capital and excites the solicitude of those who are concerned for good morals and social order. For, if a man may be made to part with one species of property by Boycotting or agitation, why not with another? If a man's title to land is as rightful as his title to his watch, what is the difference between agitation by Land

* I use the word in the usual sense in which it is used by the vulgar, and in which a Communist is understood as one who wants to divide up other people's property.

League meetings and Parliamentary filibustering to make him give up the one and agitation with a cocked pistol to make him give up the other?

But, if it be denied that land justly is, or can be, private property, if the equal rights of the whole people to the use of the elements gratuitously furnished by Nature be asserted without drawback or compromise, then the essential difference between property in land and property in things of human production is at once brought out. Then will it clearly appear not only that the denial of the right of individual property in land does not involve any menace to legitimate property rights, but that the maintenance of private property in land necessarily involves a denial of the right to all other property, and that the recognition of the claims of the landlords means a continuous robbery of capital as well as of labour.

All this will appear more and more clearly as the practical measures necessary to make land common property are proposed and discussed. These simple measures involve no harsh proceedings, no forcible dispossession, no shock to public confidence, no retrogression to a lower industrial organisation, no loaning of public money, or establishment of cumbrous commissions. Instead of doing violence to the rightful sense of property, they assert and vindicate it. The way to make land common property is simply to take rent for the common benefit. And to do this, the easy way is to abolish one tax after another, until the whole weight of taxation falls upon the value of land. When that point is reached the battle is won. The hare is caught, killed, and skinned, and to cook him will be a very easy matter. The real fight will come on the proposition to consolidate existing taxation upon land values. When that is once won, the landholders will not merely have been decisively defeated, they will have been routed; and the nature of land values will be so generally understood that to raise taxation so as to take the whole rent for common purposes will be a mere matter of course.

The political art is like the military art. It consists in combining the greatest strength against the point of least resistance. I have pointed out the way in which, in the case we are considering, this can be done. And, the more the matter is considered, the clearer and clearer will it appear that there is every practical reason, as there is every theoretical reason, why the Irish reformers should take this vantage ground of principle. To propose to put the public burdens upon the landholders is not a novel and unheard of thing against which English prejudice would run as something "new-fangled," some new invention of modern socialism. On the contrary, it is the ancient English practice. It would be but a return, in a form adapted to modern times, to the system under which English land was originally parcelled out to the predecessors of the present holders—the just system, recognised for centuries, that those who enjoy the common property should bear the common burdens. The putting of property in land in the same category as property in things produced by labour is comparatively modern. In England, as in Ireland and Scotland, as in fact among every people of whom we know anything, the land was originally treated as common property, and this recognition ran all through the feudal system. The essence of the feual system was in treating the landholder not as an owner, but as a lessee. William the Conqueror did not give away the land of England as the Church lands were given away by Henry VIII, when he divided among his sycophants the property of the people, which, after the manner of the times, had been set apart for the support of religious, educational, and charitable institutions. To every grant of land made by the Conqueror was annexed a condition which amounted to a heavy perpetual tax or rent. One of his first acts was to divide the soil of England into sixty thousand knights' fees; and thus, besides many other dues and obligations, was thrown upon the landholders the cost of providing and maintaining the army. All the long, costly wars that England fought during feudal times involved no public debt. Public debt, pauperism, and the grinding poverty of the poorer classes came in as the landholders gradually shook off the obligations on which they had received their land, an operation culminating in the abolition by the Long Parliament (re-enacted after the Restoration) of the feudal tenures, for which were substituted indirect taxes that still weigh upon the whole people. To now reverse this process, to abolish the taxes which are borne by labour and capital, and to substitute for them a tax on rent, would not be the adoption of anything new, but a simple going back to the old plan. In England, as in Ireland, the movement would appeal to the popular imagination as a demand for the re-assertion of ancient rights.

There are other most important respects in which this measure will commend itself to the English mind. The tax upon land values or rent is in all economic respects the most perfect of taxes. No political economist will deny that it combines the maximum of certainty with the minimum of loss and cost; that, unlike taxes upon capital or exchange or improvement, it does not check production or enhance prices or fall ultimately upon the consumer. And, in proposing to abolish all other taxes in favour of this theoretically perfect tax, the Land Reformers will have on their side the advantage of ideas already current, while they can bring the *argumentum ad hominem* to bear on those who might never comprehend an abstract principle. Englishmen of all classes have happily been educated up to a belief in free trade, though a very large amount of revenue is still collected from customs. Let the Land Reformers take advantage of this by proposing to carry out the doctrine of free trade to its fullest extent. If a revenue tariff is better than a protective tariff, then no tariff at all is better than a revenue tariff. Let them propose to abolish the customs duties entirely, and to abolish as well harbour dues and lighthouse dues and dock charges, and in their place to add to the tax on rent, or the value of land exclusive of improvements. Let them in the same way propose to get rid of the excise, the various licence taxes, the tax upon buildings, the onerous and unpopular income tax, etc., and to saddle all public expenses on the landlords.

This would bring home the land question to thousands and thousands who have never thought of it before; to thousands and thousands who have heretofore looked upon the land question as something peculiarly Irish, or something that related exclusively to agriculture and to farmers, and have never seen how, in various direct and indirect ways, they have to contribute to the immense sums received by the landlords as rent. It would be putting the argument in a shape in which even the most stupid could understand it. It would be directing the appeal to a spot where even the unimaginative are sensitive—the pocket. How long would a merchant or banker or manufacturer or annuitant regard as dangerous and wicked an agitation which proposed to take taxation off of him? Even the most prejudiced can be relied on to listen with patience to an argument in favour of making some one else pay what they now are paying.

Let me illustrate by a little story what I feel confident would be the effect of the policy I propose:

Once upon a time I was the Pacific-coast agent of an Eastern news association, which took advantage of an opposition telegraph company to run against the Associated Press monopoly. The association in California consisted of one strong San Francisco paper, to which telegraphic news was of much importance, and a number of interior papers, to which it was of minor importance, if of any importance at all. It became necessary to raise more money for the expenses of collecting and transmitting these dispatches, and, thinking it only fair, I assessed the increased cost to the strong metropolitan paper. The proprietor of this paper was very indignant. He appealed to the proprietors of all the other papers, and they all joined in his protest. I replied by calling a meeting. At this meeting the proprietor of the San Francisco paper led off with an indignant speech. He was seconded by several others, and evidently had the sympathy of the whole crowd. Then came my turn. I said, in effect: "Gentlemen, you can do what you please about this matter. Whatever satisfies you satisfies me. The only thing fixed is, that more money has to be raised. As this San Francisco paper pays now a much lower relative rate than you do, I thought it only fair that it should pay the increased cost. But, if you think otherwise, there is no reason in the world why you should not pay it yourselves." The debate immediately took another turn, and in a few minutes my action was endorsed by a unanimous vote, for the San Francisco man was so disgusted by the way his supporters left him that he would not vote at all.

Now, that is just about what will happen to the English landlords if the question be put in the way I propose. The British landowners are in numbers but an insignificant minority. And, the more they protested against the injustice of having to pay all the taxes, the quicker would the public mind realize the essential injustice of private property in land, the quicker would the majority of the people come to see that the landowners ought not only to pay all the taxes, but a good deal more besides. Once put the question in such a way that the British working man will realize that he pays two prices for his ale and half a dozen prices for his tobacco, because a landowners' Parliament in the time of Charles II. shook off their ancient dues to the State, and imposed them in indirect taxation on him; once bring to the attention of the well-to-do Englishman, who grunts as he pays his income tax, the question as to whether the landowner who draws his income from property that of natural right belongs to the whole people ought not to pay it instead of him, and it will not be long before the absurd injustice of allowing rent to be appropriated by individuals will be thoroughly understood. This is a very different thing from asking the British taxpayer to buy out the Irish landlord for the sake of the Irish peasant.

I have been speaking as though all landholders would resist the change which would sacrifice their special interests to the larger interests of society. But I am satisfied that to think this is to do landholders a great injustice. For landholders as a class are not more stupid nor more selfish than any other class. And as they saw, as they must see, as the discussion progresses, that they also would be the gainers in the great social change which would abolish poverty and elevate the very lowest classes above the want, the misery, the vice, and degradation in which they are now plunged, there are many landowners who would join heartily and unreservedly in the effort to bring this change about. This I know, not merely because my reading and observation both teach me that low, narrow views of self-interest are not the strongest of human motives, but because I know that to-day among those who see the truth I have here tried to set forth, and who would carry out the reform I have proposed, are many landowners.* And, if they be earnest men, I appeal to landholders as confidently as to any other class. There is that in a great truth that can raise a human soul above the mists of selfishness.

The course which I suggest is the only course which can be logically based on principle. It has everything to commend it. It will concentrate the greatest strength against the least resistance. And it will be on the right line. Every step gained will be an advance toward the ultimate goal; every step gained will make easier the next.

XII.

In speaking with special reference to the case of Ireland, I have, so far as general principles are concerned, been using it as a stalking-horse. In discussing the Irish land question, we really discuss the most vital of American questions. And if we of the United States cannot see the beam in our own eye, save by looking at the mote in our neighbour's, then let us look at the mote; and let us take counsel together how *he* may get it out. For, at least, we shall in this way learn how we may deal with our own case when we wake up to the consciousness of it.

And never had the parable of the mote and the beam a better illustration than in the attitude of so many Americans towards this Irish land question. *We* denounce the Irish land

---

* Among the warm friends my book "Progress and Poverty" has found are many landholders—some of them large landholders. As types I may mention the names of D. A. Learnard, of San Joaquin, a considerable farmer, who had no sooner read it than he sent for a dozen copies to circulate among his neighbours; Hiram Tubbs, of San Francisco, the owner of much valuable real estate in and near that city; and Sir George Grey, of New Zealand, the owner of a good deal of land in that colony, of which he was formerly governor, as well, as I understand, of valuable estates in England.

system! *We* express our sympathy with Ireland! *We* tender our advice by congressional and legislative resolution to our British brethren across the sea! Truly our indignation is cheap, and our sympathy is cheap, and our advice is very, very cheap! For what are *we* doing? Extending over new soil the very institution that to them descended from a ruder and a darker time. With what conscience can we lecture them? With all power in the hands of the people, with institutions yet plastic, with millions of virgin acres yet to settle, it should be ours to do more than vent denunciation, and express sympathy, and give advice. It should be ours to show the way. This we have not done; this we do not do. Out in our new States may be seen the growth of a system of cultivation worse in its social effects than that which prevails in Ireland. In Ireland the labourer has some sort of a home, and enjoys some of the family affections. In these great "wheat-manufacturing" districts the labourer is a nomad, his home is in his blankets, which he carries around with him. And in our large cities may we not see misery of the same kind as exists in Ireland? If it is less in amount, is it not merely because our country is yet newer; because we have yet a wide territory and a sparse population—conditions past which our progress is rapidly carrying us? As for evictions, is it an unheard-of thing, even in New York, for families to be turned out of their homes because they cannot pay the rent? Are there not many acres in this country from which those who made homes have been driven by sheriffs' posses, and even by troops?

And the men on the other side of the Atlantic who vainly imagine that they may settle the great question now pressing upon them by free trade in land, or tenant-right, or some mild device for establishing a peasant proprietary—they may learn something about their own case if they will turn their eyes to us.

We have had free trade in land; we have had in our American farmer, owning his own acres, using his own capital, and working with his own hands, something far better than peasant proprietorship. We have had, what no legislation can give the people of Great Britain, vast areas of virgin soil. We have had all of these under democratic institutions. Yet we have here social disease of precisely the same kind as that which exists in Ireland and England. And the reason is that we have had here precisely the same cause—that we have made land private property So long as this exists, our democratic institutions are vain, our pretence of equality but cruel irony, our public schools can but sow the seeds of discontent. So long as this exists, material progress can but force the masses of our people into a harder and more hopeless slavery. Until we in some way make the land, what Nature intended it to be, common property, until we in some way secure to every child born among us his natural birthright, we have not established the Republic in any sense worthy of the name, and we cannot establish the Republic. Its foundations are quicksand.

XIII.

Imagine an island girt with ocean; imagine a little world swimming in space. Put on it, in imagination, human beings. Let them divide the land, share and share alike, as individual property. At first, while population is sparse, and industrial processes rude and primitive, this will work well enough.

Turn away the eyes of the mind for a moment, let time pass, and look again. Some families will have died out, some have greatly multiplied: on the whole, population will have largely increased, and even supposing there have been no important inventions or improvements in the productive arts, the increase in population, by causing the division of labour, will have made industry more complex. During this time some of these people will have been careless, generous, improvident; some will have been thrifty and grasping. Some of them will have devoted much of their powers to thinking of how they themselves and the things they see around them came to be, to inquiries and speculations as to what there is in the universe beyond their little island or their little world, to making poems, painting pictures, or writing books; to noting the differences in rocks and trees, and shrubs and grasses; to classifying beasts and birds and fishes and insects—to the doing, in short, of all of the many things which add so largely to the sum of human knowledge and human happiness, without much or any gain of wealth to the doer. Others, again, will have devoted all their energies to the extending of their possessions. What, then, shall we see, land having been all this time treated as private property? Clearly, we shall see that the primitive equality has given way to inequality. Some will have very much more than one of the original shares into which the land was divided; very many will have no land at all. Suppose that, in all things save this, our little island or our little world is Utopia, yet inequality in the ownership of land will have produced poverty and virtual slavery.

For the people we have supposed are human beings—that is to say, in their physical natures at least, they are animals who can only live on land and by aid of the products of land. They may make machines which will enable them to float on the sea, or perhaps to fly in the air, but to build and equip these machines they must have land and the products of land, and must constantly come back to land. Therefore, those who own the land must be the masters of the rest. Thus, if one man has come to own all the land, he is their absolute master, even to life or death. If they can only live on the land on his terms, then they can only live on his terms, for without land they cannot live. They are his absolute slaves, and so long as his ownership is acknowledged, if they want to live, they must do in everything as he wills.

If, however, the concentration of landownership has not gone so far as to make one or a very few men the owners of all the land—if there are still so many landowners that there is competition between them as well as between those who have only their labour—then the terms on which these non-landholders can live will seem more like free contract. But it will not be free contract. Land can yield no wealth without the application of labour; labour can produce no wealth without land. These are the two equally necessary factors of production. Yet, to say that they are equally necessary factors of production is not to say that, in the making of contracts as to how the results of production are divided, the possessors of these two meet on equal terms. For the nature of these two factors is very different. Land is a natural element; the human being must have his stomach filled every few hours. Land can exist without labour, but labour cannot exist without land. If I own a piece of land, I can let it lay idle for a year or for years, and it will eat nothing. But the labourer must eat every day, and his family must eat. And so, in the making of terms between them, the landowner has an immense advantage over the labourer. It is on the side of the labourer that the intense pressure of competition comes, for in his case it is competition urged by hunger. And, further than this: As population increases, as the competition for the use of the land becomes more and more intense, so are the owners of land enabled to get for the use of their land a larger and larger part of the wealth which labour exerted upon it produces. That is to say, the value of land steadily rises. Now, this steady rise in the value of land brings about a confident expectation of future increase of value, which produces among landowners all the effects of a combination to hold for higher prices. Thus there is a constant tendency to force mere labourers to take less and less or to give more and more (put it which way you please, it amounts to the same thing) of the products of their work for the opportunity to work. And thus, in the very nature of things, we should see on our little island or our little world that, after a time had passed, some of the people would be able to take and enjoy a superabundance of all the fruits of labour without doing any labour at all, while others would be forced to work the livelong day for a pitiful living.

But let us introduce another element into the supposition. Let us suppose great discoveries and inventions—such as the steam-engine, the power-loom, the Bessemer process, the reaping-machine, and the thousand-and-one labour-saving devices that are such a marked feature of our era. What would be the result?

Manifestly, the effect of all such discoveries and inventions is to increase the power of labour in producing wealth—to enable the same amount of wealth to be produced by less labour, or a greater amount with the same labour. But none of them lessen or can lessen the necessity for land. Until we can discover some way of making something out of nothing—and that is so far beyond our powers as to be absolutely unthinkable—there is no possible discovery or invention which can lessen the dependence of labour upon land. And, this being the case, the effect of these labour-saving devices, land being the private property of some, would simply be to increase the proportion of the wealth produced that landowners could demand for the use of their land. The ultimate effect of these discoveries and inventions would be not to benefit the labourer, but to make him more dependent.

And, since we are imagining conditions, imagine labour-saving inventions to go to the farthest imaginable point, that is to say, to perfection. What then? Why, then, the necessity for labour being done away with, all the wealth that the land could produce would go entire to the landowners. None of it whatever could be claimed by any one else. For the labourers there would be no use at all. If they continued to exist, it would be merely as paupers on the bounty of the landowners!

XIV.

In the effects upon the distribution of wealth, of making land private property, we may thus see an explanation of that paradox presented by modern progress. The perplexing phenomena of deepening want with increasing wealth, of labour rendered more dependent and helpless by the very introduction of labour-saving machinery, are the inevitable result of natural laws as fixed and certain as the law of gravitation. Private property in land is the primary cause of the monstrous inequalities which are developing in modern society. It is this, and not any miscalculation of Nature in bringing into the world more mouths than she can feed, that gives rise to that tendency of wages to a minimum—that "iron law of wages," as the Germans call it—that, in spite of all advances in productive power, compels the labouring classes to the least return on which they will consent to live. It is this that produces all those phenomena that are so often attributed to the conflict of labour and capital. It is this that condemns Irish peasants to rags and hunger, that produces the pauperism of England and the tramps of America. It is this that makes the almshouse and the penitentiary the marks of what we call high civilization; that in the midst of schools and churches degrades and brutalizes men, crushes the sweetness out of womanhood and the joy out of childhood. It is this that makes lives that might be a blessing a pain and a curse, and every year drives more and more to seek unbidden refuge in the gates of death. For, a permanent tendency to inequality once set up, all the forces of progress tend to greater and greater inequality.

All this is contrary to Nature. The poverty and misery, the vice and degradation that spring from the unequal distribution of wealth, are not the results of natural law; they spring from our defiance of natural law. They are the fruits of our refusal to obey the supreme law of justice. It is because we rob the child of his birthright; because we make the bounty which the Creator intended for all the exclusive property of some, that these things come upon us, and, though advancing and advancing, we chase but the mirage.

When, lit by lightning-flash or friction amid dry grasses, the consuming flames of fire first flung their lurid glow into the face of man, how must he have started back in affright! When he first stood by the shores of the sea, how must its waves have said to him, "Thus far shalt thou go, but no farther!" Yet, as he learned to use them, fire became his most useful servant, the sea his easiest highway. The most destructive element of which we know—that which for ages and ages seemed the very thunderbolt of the angry gods—is, as we are now beginning to learn, fraught for us with untold powers of usefulness. Already it enables us to annihilate space in our messages, to illuminate the night with new suns; and its uses are only beginning. And throughout all Nature, as far as we can see, whatever is potent for evil is potent for good. "Dirt," said Lord Brougham, "is matter in the wrong place." And so the squalor and vice and misery that abound in the very heart of our civilization are but results of the misapplication of forces in their nature most elevating.

I doubt not that, whichever way a man may turn to inquire of Nature, he will come upon adjustments which will arouse not merely his wonder, but his gratitude. Yet what has most impressed me with the feeling that the laws of Nature are the laws of beneficent intelligence is what I see of the social possibilities involved in the law of rent. Rent* springs from natural causes. It arises, as society develops, from the differences in natural opportunities and the differences in the distribution of population. It increases with the division of labour, with the advance of the arts, with the progress of invention. And thus, by virtue of a law impressed upon the very nature of things, has the Creator provided that the natural advance of mankind shall be an advance toward equality, an advance toward co-operation, an advance toward a social state in which not even the weakest need be crowded to the wall, in which even for the unfortunate and the cripple there may be ample provision. For this revenue, which arises from the common property, which represents not the creation of value by the individual, but the creation by the community as a whole, which increases just as society develops, affords a common fund, which, properly used, tends constantly to equalise conditions, to open the largest opportunities for all, and to utterly banish want or the fear of want.

The squalid poverty that festers in the heart of our civilization, the vice and crime and degradation and ravening greed that flow from it, are the results of a treatment of land that ignores the simple law of justice, a law so clear and plain that it is universally recognised by the veriest savages. What is by nature the common birthright of all, we have made the exclusive property of individuals; what is by natural law the common fund, from which common wants should be met, we give to a few that they may lord it over their fellows. And so some are gorged while some go hungry, and more is wasted than would suffice to keep all in luxury.

In this nineteenth century, among any people who have begun to utilise the forces and methods of modern production, there is no necessity for want. There is no good reason why even the poorest should not have all the comforts, all the luxuries, all the opportunities for culture, all the gratifications of

* I, of course, use the word "rent" in its economic, not in its common sense, meaning by it what is commonly called ground rent.

refined taste that only the richest now enjoy. There is no reason why any one should be compelled to long and monotonous labour. Did invention and discovery stop to-day, the forces of production are ample for this. What hampers production is the unnatural inequality in distribution. And, with just distribution, invention and discovery would only have begun.

Appropriate rent in the way I propose, and speculative rent would be at once destroyed. The dogs in the manger who are now holding so much land they have no use for, in order to extract a high price from those who do want to use it, would be at once choked off, and land from which labour and capital are now debarred under penalty of a heavy fine would be thrown open to improvement and use. The incentive to land monopoly would be gone. Population would spread where it is now too dense, and become denser where it is now too sparse.

Appropriate rent in this way, and not only would natural opportunities be thus opened to labour and capital, but all the taxes which now weigh upon production and rest upon the consumer could be abolished. The demand for labour would increase, wages would rise, every wheel of production would be set in motion.

Appropriate rent in this way, and the present expenses of government would be at once very much reduced—reduced directly by the saving in the present cumbrous and expensive schemes of taxation, reduced indirectly by the diminution in pauperism and in crime. This simplification in governmental machinery, this elevation of moral tone which would result, would make it possible for government to assume the running of railroads, telegraphs, and other businesses which, being in their nature monopolies, cannot, as experience is showing, be safely left in the hands of private individuals and corporations. In short, losing its character as a repressive agency, government could thus gradually pass into an administrative agency of the great co-operative association—society.

For, appropriate rent in this way, and there would be at once a large surplus over and above what are now considered the legitimate expenses of government. We could divide this, if we wanted to, among the whole community, share and share alike. Or we could give every boy a small capital for a start when he came of age, every girl a dower, every widow an annuity, every aged person a pension, out of this common estate. Or we could do with our great common fund many, many things that would be for the common benefit, many, many things that would give to the poorest what even the richest cannot now enjoy. We could establish free libraries, lectures, museums, art-galleries, observatories, gymnasiums, baths, parks, theatres; we could line our roads with fruit-trees, and make our cities clean and wholesome and beautiful; we could conduct experiments, and offer rewards for inventions, and throw them open to public use.*

Think of the enormous wastes that now go on: The waste of false revenue systems, which hamper production and bar exchange, which fine a man for erecting a building where none stood before, or for making two blades of grass grow where there was but one. The waste of unemployed labour, of idle machinery, of those periodical depressions of industry, almost as destructive as war. The waste entailed by poverty, and the vice, and crime, and thriftlessness, and drunkenness that spring from it; the waste entailed by that greed of gain that is its shadow, and which makes business in large part but a masked war; the waste entailed by the fret and worry about the mere physical necessities of existence, to which so many of us are condemned; the waste entailed by ignorance, by cramped and undeveloped faculties, by the turning of human beings into mere machines!

Think of these enormous wastes, and of the others which, like these, are due to the fundamental wrong which produces an unjust distribution of wealth, and distorts the natural development of society, and you will begin to see what a higher, purer, richer civilization would be made possible by the simple measure that will assert natural rights. You will begin to see how, even if no one but the present landholders were to be considered, this would be the greatest boon that could be vouchsafed them by society, and that, for them to fight it, would be as if the dog with a tin kettle tied to his tail should snap at the hand that offered to free him. Even the greatest landlord! As for such landlords as our working farmers and homestead owners, the slightest discussion would show them that they had everything to gain by the change. But even such landholders as the Duke of Westminster and the Astors would be gainers. For it is of the very nature of injustice that it really profits no one.

This we may know certainly, this we may hold to confidently: that which is unjust can really profit no one; that which is just can really harm no one. Though all other lights move and circle, this is the pole-star by which we may safely steer.

* A million dollars spent in premiums and experiments would, in all probability, make aërial navigation an accomplished fact.

XV.

When we think of the civilization that might be, how poor and pitiful, how little better than utter barbarism seems this civilization of which we boast! Even here, where it has had the freest field and fullest development! Even here!

This is a broad land and a rich land. How wide it is, how rich it is, how the fifty millions of us already here are but beginning to scratch it, a man cannot begin to realise till he does some thousands of miles of travelling over it. There are a school and a church and a newspaper in every hamlet; we have no privileged orders, no legacies of antiquated institutions, no strong and covertly hostile neighbours, who in fancy or reality oblige us to keep up great standing armies. We have had the experience of all other nations to guide us in selecting what is good and rejecting what is bad. In politics, in religion, in science, in mechanism, everything shows the latest improvements. We think we stand, and in fact we do stand, in the very van of civilization. Food here is cheaper, wages higher, than anywhere else. There is here a higher average of education, of intelligence, of material comfort, and of individual opportunity, than among any other of the great civilized nations. Here modern civilization is at its very best. Yet even here!

Last winter I was in San Francisco. There are in San Francisco citizens who can build themselves houses that cost a million and a half; citizens who can give each of their children two millions of registered United States bonds for a Christmas present; citizens who can send their wives to Paris to keep house there, or rather to "keep palace," in a style which outdoes the lavishness of Russian grand dukes. There are, also, in San Francisco other citizens. Last winter I could hardly walk a block without meeting a citizen begging for ten cents. And, when a charity fund was raised to give work, with pick and shovel, to such as would rather work than beg, the applications were so numerous that, to make the charity fund go as far as possible, one set of men was discharged after having been given a few days' work, in order to make room for another set.

Last summer, on the plains, I took from its tired mother, and held in my arms, a little sun-browned baby, the youngest of a family of the sturdy and keen Western New England stock, who alone in their two waggons had travelled near three thousand miles looking for some place to locate and finding none, and who were now returning to where the father and his biggest boy could go to work on a railroad, what they had got by the sale of their Nebraska farm all gone. And I walked awhile by the side of long, lank South-western men who, after similar fruitless journeyings way up into Washington territory, were going back to the Choctaw Nation.

This winter I have been in New York. New York is the greatest and richest of American cities—the third city of the modern world, and moving steadily toward the first place. This is a time of great prosperity. Never before were so many goods sold, so much business done. Real estate is advancing with big jumps, and within the last few months many fortunes have been made in buying and selling vacant lots. Landlords nearly everywhere are demanding increased rents; asking in some of the business quarters an increase of three hundred per cent. Money is so plenty that government four per cents. sell for 114, and a bill is passing Congress for refunding the maturing national debt at three per cent. per annum, a rate that awhile ago in California was not thought exorbitant per month. All sorts of shares and bonds have been going up and up. You can sell almost anything if you give it a high-sounding corporate name and issue well-printed shares of stock.

Nevertheless, prosperous as are these times, citizens of the United States beg you on the streets for ten cents and five cents, and although you know that there are in this city two hundred charitable societies, although you realise that on general principles to give money in this way is to do evil rather than good, you are afraid to refuse them when you read of men in this great city freezing to death and starving to death. Prosperous as are these times, women are making overalls for sixty cents a dozen, and you can hire citizens for trivial sums to parade up and down the streets all day with advertising placards on their backs. I get on a horse-car and ride with the driver. He is evidently a sober, steady man, as intelligent as a man can be who drives a horse-car all the time he is not asleep or eating his meals. He tells me he has a wife and four children. He gets home (if a couple of rooms can be called a home) at two o'clock in the morning; he has to be back on his car at nine. Sunday he has two hours more. He gets one dollar and seventy-five cents per day. I say to him that it must be pretty hard to pay rent and keep six persons on one dollar and seventy-five cents a-day. He says it is; that he has been trying for a month to get enough ahead to buy a new pair of shoes, but he hasn't yet succeeded. I ask why he does not leave such a job. He says, "What can I do? There are a thousand men ready to step into my place!" And so, in this time of prosperity, he is chained to his car.

Our Napoleon of Wall Street, our Charlemagne of railroads, who came to this city with nothing but a new kind of mouse-trap in a mahogany box, but who now, though yet in the vigour of his prime, counts his wealth by hundreds of millions, if it can be counted at all, is interviewed by a reporter just as he is about to step aboard his palace-car for a grand combination expedition into the South-west. He descants upon the services he is rendering in welding into one big machine a lot of smaller machines, in uniting into one vast railroad empire the divided railroad kingdoms. He likewise descants upon the great prosperity of the whole country. Everybody is prosperous and contented he says: there is, of course, a good deal of misery in the big cities, but, then, there always is!

But not alone in the great cities. I ride on the Hudson River Railroad on a bitter cold day, and from one of the pretty towns with Dutch names gets in a constable with a prisoner, whom he is to take to the Albany penitentiary. In this case justice has been swift enough, for the crime, the taking of a shovel, has only been committed a few hours before. Such coat as the man has he keeps buttoned up, even in the hot car, for, the constable says, he has no underclothes at all. He stole the shovel to get to the penitentiary, where it is warm. The constable says they have lots of such cases, and that even in these good times these pretty country towns are infested with such tramps.

Is it real advance in civilization which, on the one hand, produces these great captains of industry, and, on the other, these social outcasts?

This is a most highly civilized community, yet every lower window has to be barred, every door locked and bolted; even door-mats, not worth twenty-five cents, you will see chained to the steps. Stop for a moment in a crowd and your watch is gone as if by magic; shirt-studs are taken from their owners' bosoms, and ear-rings cut from ladies' ears. Even a standing army of policemen do not prevent highway robbery; there are populous districts that to walk through after nightfall is a risk, and where you have far more need to go armed and to be wary than in the backwoods. There are dens into which men are lured only to be drugged and robbed, sometimes to be murdered All the resources of science and inventive genius are exhausted in making burglar-proof strong-rooms and safes, yet, as the steel plate becomes thicker and harder, so does the burglar's tool become keener. If the combination lock cannot be picked, it is blown open. If not a crack large enough for the introduction of powder is left, then the air-pump is applied and a vacuum is created. So that those who in the heart of civilization would guard their treasures safely must come back to the most barbarous device, and either themselves, or by proxy, sleeplessly stand guard. What sort of a civilization is this? In what does civilization essentially consist if not in civility—that is to say, in respect for the rights of person and of property?

Yet this is not all, nor the worst. These are but the grosser forms of that spirit that in the midst of civilization compels every one to stand on guard. What is the maxim of business intercourse among the most highly respectable classes? That if you are swindled it will be your own fault; that you must treat every man you have dealings with as though he but wanted the chance to cheat and rob you. *Caveat emptor!* "Let the buyer beware." If a man steal a few dollars he may stand a chance of going to the penitentiary. I read the other day of a man who was sent to the penitentiary for stealing four cents from a horse-car company. But, if he steal a million by business methods, he is courted and flattered, even though he steal the poor little savings which washer-women and sewing-girls have brought to him in trust, even though he rob widows and orphans of the security which dead men have struggled and stinted to provide.

This is a most Christian city. There are churches and churches. All sorts of churches, where are preached all sorts of religions, save that which once in Galilee taught the arrant socialistic doctrine that it is easier for a camel to pass through the eye of a needle than for a rich man to enter the kingdom of God; all save that which once in Jerusalem drove the money-changers from the temple. Churches restful to the very eye, in which the weary and heavy laden can join in the worship of their Creator for no larger an admission fee than it costs on the Bowery to see the bearded lady or the Zulu giant eight feet high. And then there are mission churches, run expressly for poor people, where it does not cost a cent. There are, in fact, more churches than there are people who care to attend them. And there are likewise Sunday schools, and big religious "book concerns," and tract societies, and societies for spreading the light of the Gospel among the heathen in foreign parts.

Yet, land a heathen on the Battery with money in his pocket, and he will be robbed of the last cent of it before he is a day older. "By their fruits shall ye know them." I wonder whether they who send missionaries to the heathen ever read the daily papers. I think I could take a file of these newspapers, and from their daily chroniclings match anything that could be told in the same period of any heathen community—at least, of any heathen community in a like state of peace and prosperity.

I do not say that such things are because of civilization, or because of Christianity. On the contrary, I point to them as inconsistent with civilization, as incompatible with Christianity. They show that our civilization is one-sided and cannot last as at present based; they show that our so-called Christian communities are not Christian at all. I believe a civilization is possible in which all could be civilized—in which such things could be impossible. But it must be a civilization based on justice and acknowledging the equal rights of all to natural opportunities. I believe that there is in true Christianity a power to regenerate the world. But it must be a Christianity that attacks vested wrongs, not that spurious thing that defends them. The religion which allies itself with injustice to preach down the natural aspirations of the masses is worse than atheism.

XVI.

There are those who may look on this little book as very radical, in the bad sense they attach to the word. They mistake. This is, in the true sense of the word, a most conservative little book. I do not appeal to prejudice and passion. I appeal to intelligence. I do not incite to strife; I seek to prevent strife.

That the civilized world is on the verge of the most tremendous struggle, which, according to the frankness and sagacity with which it is met, will be a struggle of ideas or a struggle of actual physical force, calling upon all the potent agencies of destruction which modern invention has discovered, every sign of the times portends. The voices that proclaim the eve of revolution are in the air. Steam and electricity are not merely transporting goods and carrying messages. They are everywhere changing social and industrial organization; they are everywhere stimulating thought, and arousing new hopes and fears, and desires and passions; they are everywhere breaking down the barriers that have separated men, and integrating nations into one vast organism, through which the same pulses throb and the same nerves tingle.

The present situation in Great Britain is full of dangers—of dangers graver and nearer than those who there are making history are likely to see. For the moment the forces of reaction triumph. Davitt is snatched to prison; a "Liberal" Government carries coercion by a tremendous majority, and the most despotic powers are invoked to make possible the eviction of Irish peasants. The order of Warsaw is to reign in Ireland, and the upholders of ancient wrong deem it secure again, as the wave that was mounting seems sweeping back. Let them wait a little and they will see. For again the wave will mount, and higher and higher, and soon the white foam will seethe and hiss on its toppling crest. It is not true conservatism which cries "Peace! peace!" when there is no peace; which, like the ostrich, sticks its head in the sand and fancies itself secure; which would compromise matters by putting more coal in the furnace, and hanging heavier weights on the safety-valve! That alone is true conservatism which would look facts in the face, which would reconcile opposing forces on the only basis on which reconciliation is possible—that of justice.

I speak again of Great Britain, but I speak with reference to the whole modern world. The true nature of the inevitable conflict with which modern civilization is everywhere beginning to throb can, it seems to me, best be seen in the United States, and in the newer States even more clearly than in the older States. That intelligent Englishmen imagine that in the democratization of political institutions, in free trade in land, or in peasant proprietorship, can be found any solution of the difficulties which are confronting them, is because they do not see what may be seen in the United States by whoever will look. That intelligent Americans imagine that by these questions which are so menacingly presenting themselves in Europe their peace is to be unvexed, is because they shut their eyes to what is going on around them, because they attribute to themselves and their institutions what is really due to conditions now rapidly passing away—to the sparseness of population and the cheapness of land. Yet it is here, in this American Republic, that the true nature of that inevitable conflict now rapidly approaching which must determine the fate of modern civilization may be most clearly seen.

We have here abolished all hereditary privileges and legal distinctions of class. Monarchy, aristocracy, prelacy, we have swept them all away. We have carried mere political democracy to its ultimate. Every child born in the United States may aspire to be President. Every man, even though he be a tramp or a pauper, has a vote, and one man's vote counts for as much as any other man's vote. Before the law all citizens are absolutely equal. In the name of the people all laws run.

They are the source of all power, the fountain of all honour. In their name and by their will all government is carried on; the highest officials are but their servants. Primogeniture and entail we have abolished wherever they existed. We have and have had free trade in land. We started with something infinitely better than any scheme of peasant proprietorship which it is possible to carry into effect in Great Britain. We have had for our public domain the best part of an immense continent. We have had the preëmption law and the homestead law. It has been our boast that here every one who wished it could have a farm. We have had full liberty of speech and of the press. We have not merely common schools, but high schools and universities, open to all who may choose to attend. Yet here the same social difficulties apparent on the other side of the Atlantic are beginning to appear. It is already clear that our democracy is a vain pretence, our make-believe of equality a sham and a fraud.

Already are the sovereign people becoming but a *roi fainéant*, like the Merovingian kings of France, like the Mikados of Japan. The shadow of power is theirs; but the substance of power is being grasped and wielded by the bandit chiefs of the stock exchange, the robber leaders who organize politics into machines. In any matter in which they are interested, the little finger of the great corporations is thicker than the loins of the people. Is it sovereign States or is it railroad corporations that are really represented in the elective Senate which we have substituted for an hereditary House of Lords? Where is the count or marquis or duke in Europe who wields such power as is wielded by such simple citizens as our Stanfords, Goulds, and Vanderbilts? What does legal eqality amount to, when the fortunes of some citizens can only be estimated in hundreds of millions, and other citizens have nothing? What does the suffrage amount to when, under threat of discharge from employment, citizens can be forced to vote as their employers dictate? when votes can be bought on election day for a few dollars apiece? If there are citizens so dependent that they must vote as their employers wish, so poor that a few dollars on election day seem to them more than any higher consideration, then giving them votes simply adds to the political power of wealth, and universal suffrage becomes the surest basis for the establishment of tyranny.

Even if universal history did not teach the lesson, it is in the United States already becoming very evident that political equality can only continue to exist upon a basis of social equality; that where the disparity in the distribution of wealth increases, political democracy only makes easier the concentration of power, and must inevitably lead to tyranny and anarchy. And it is already evident that there is nothing in political democracy, nothing in popular education, nothing in any of our American institutions, to prevent the most enormous disparity in the distribution of wealth. Nowhere in the world are such great fortunes growing up as in the United States. Considering that the average income of the working masses of our people is only a few hundred dollars a year, a fortune of a million dollars is a monstrous thing—a more monstrous and dangerous thing under a democratic government than anywhere else. Yet fortunes of ten and twelve million dollars are with us ceasing to be noticeable. We already have citizens whose wealth can only be estimated in hundreds of millions, and before the end of the century, if present tendencies continue, we are likely to have fortunes estimated in thousands of millions—such monstrous fortunes as the world has never seen since the growth of similar fortunes ate out the heart of Rome. And the necessary correlative of the growth of such fortunes is the impoverishment and loss of independence on the part of the masses. These great aggregations of wealth are like great trees, which strike deep roots and spread wide branches, and which, by sucking up the moisture from the soil and intercepting the sunshine, stunt and kill the vegetation around them. When a capital of a million dollars comes into competition with capitals of thousands of dollars, the smaller capitalists must be driven out of the business or destroyed. With great capital nothing can compete save great capital. Hence, every aggregation of wealth increases the tendency to the aggregation of wealth, and decreases the possibility of the employee ever becoming more than an employee, compelling him to compete with his fellows as to who will work cheapest for the great capitalist—a competition that can have but one result, that of forcing wages to the minimum at which the supply of labour can be kept up. Where we are is not so important as in what direction we are going, and in the United States all tendencies are clearly in this direction. A while ago, and any journeyman shoemaker could set up in business for himself with the savings of a few months. But now the operative shoemaker could not in a lifetime save enough from his wages to go into business for himself. And, now that great capital has entered agriculture, it must be with the same results. The large farmer, who can buy the latest machinery at the lowest cash prices and use it to the best advantage, who can run a straight furrow for miles, who can make special rates with railroad companies, take advantage of the market, and sell in large lots for the least commission, must drive out the small farmer of the early American type just as the shoe factory has driven out the journeyman shoemaker. And this is going on to-day.

There is nothing unnatural in this. On the contrary, it is in the highest degree natural. Social development is in accordance with certain immutable laws. And the law of development, whether it be the development of a solar system, of the tiniest organism, or of a human society, is the law of integration. It is in obedience to this law—a law evidently as all-compelling as the law of gravitation—that these new agencies, which so powerfully stimulate social growth, tend to the specialization and interdependence of industry. It is in obedience to this law that the factory is superseding the independent mechanic, the large farm is swallowing up the little one, the big store shutting up the small one, that corporations are arising that dwarf the State, and that population tends more and more to concentrate in cities. Men must work together in larger and in more closely-related groups. Production must be on a greater scale. The only question is, whether the relation in which men are thus drawn together and compelled to act together shall be the natural relation of interdependence in equality, or in the unnatural relation of dependence upon a master. If the one, then may civilization advance in what is evidently the natural order, each step leading to a higher step. If the other, then what Nature has intended as a blessing becomes a curse, and a condition of inequality is produced which will inevitably destroy civilization. Every new invention but hastens the catastrophe.

Now, all this we may deduce from natural laws as fixed and certain as the law of gravitation. And all this we may see going on to-day. This is the reason why modern progress, great as it has been, fails to relieve poverty; this is the secret of the increasing discontent which pervades every civilized country. Under present conditions, with land treated as private property, material progress is developing two diverse tendencies, two opposing currents. On the one side, the tendency of increasing population and of all improvement in the arts of production is to build up enormous fortunes, to wipe out the intermediate classes, and to crowd down the masses to a level of lower wages and greater dependence. On the other hand, by bringing men closer together, by stimulating thought, by creating new wants, by arousing new ambitions, the tendency of modern progress is to make the masses discontented with their condition, to feel bitterly its injustice. The result can be predicted just as certainly as the result can be predicted when two trains are rushing toward each other on the same track.

This thing is absolutely certain: Private property in land blocks the way of advancing civilization. The two cannot long co-exist. Either private property in land must be abolished, or, as has happened again and again in the history of mankind, civilization must again turn back in anarchy and bloodshed. Let the remaining years of the nineteenth century bear me witness. Even now, I believe, the inevitable struggle has begun. It is not conservatism which would ignore such a tremendous fact. It is the blindness that invites destruction. He that is truly conservative let him look the facts in the face; let him speak frankly and dispassionately. This is *the* duty of the hour. For, when a great social question presses for settlement, it is only for a little while that the voice of Reason can be heard. The masses of men hardly think at any time. It is difficult even in sober moments to get them to calmly reason. But when passion is roused, then they are like a herd of stampeded bulls. I do not fear that present social adjustments can continue. That is impossible. What I fear is that the dams may hold till the flood rises to fury. What I fear is that dogged resistance on the one side may kindle a passionate sense of wrong on the other. What I fear are the demagogues and the accidents.

The present condition of all civilized countries is that of increasingly unstable equilibrium. In steam and electricity, and all the countless inventions which they typify, mighty forces have entered the world. If rightly used, they are our servants, more potent to do our bidding than the genii of Arabian story. If wrongly used, they, too, must turn to monsters of destruction. They require and will compel great social changes. That we may already see. Operating under social institutions which are based on natural justice, which acknowledge the equal rights of all to the material opportunities of nature, their elevating power will be equally exerted, and industrial organization will pass naturally into that of a vast co-operative society. Operating under social institutions which deny natural justice by treating land as private property, their power is unequally exerted, and tends, by producing inequality, to engender forces that will tear and rend and shatter. The old bottles cannot hold the new wine. This is the ferment which throughout the civilized world is everywhere beginning.

"IN HOC SIGNO VINCES."

"THE LAND, OF NATURAL RIGHT, THE COMMON PROPERTY OF THE WHOLE PEOPLE."

The Irish land question is not a mere local question; it is a universal question. It involves the great problem of the distribution of wealth, which is everywhere forcing itself upon attention.

It cannot be settled by measures which in their nature can have but local application. It can only be settled by measures which in their nature will apply everywhere as readily as in Ireland.

It cannot be settled by half-way measures. It can only be settled by the acknowledgment of equal rights to land. Upon this basis it can be settled easily and permanently.

TO THE MEN OF IRELAND.

If the Irish reformers take this ground, they will make their fight the common fight of all the peoples; they will concentrate strength and divide opposition. They will turn the flank of the system that oppresses them, and awake the struggle in its very intrenchments. They will rouse against it a force that is like the force of rising tides.

What I urge the men of Ireland to do is to proclaim, without limitation or evasion, that the land, of NATURAL RIGHT, is the common property of the whole people, and to propose practical measures which will recognise this right in Great Britain as well as in Ireland.

TO THE MEN OF AMERICA.

What I urge the Land Leagues of the United States to do is to announce this great principle as of universal application; to give their movement a reference to America as well as to Ireland; to broaden and deepen and strengthen it by making it a movement for the regeneration of the world—a movement which shall concentrate and give shape to aspirations that are stirring among all nations.

Ask not for Ireland mere charity or sympathy. Let her call be the call of fraternity: "For yourselves, O brothers, as well as for us!" Let her rallying cry awake all who slumber, and rouse to a common struggle all who are oppressed. Let it breathe not old hates; let it ring and echo with the new hope!

In many lands her sons are true to her; under many skies her daughters burn with the love of her. Lo! the ages bring their opportunity. Let those who would honour her carry her banner to the front!

The harp and the shamrock, the golden sunburst on the field of living green! emblems of a country without nationality; standard of a people down-trodden and oppressed! The hour has come when they may lead the van of the great world-struggle. Types of harmony and of ever-springing hope of light and of life! The hour has come when they may stand for something far higher than local patriotism; something grander than national independence. The hour has come when they may stand forth to speak the world's hope, to lead the world's advance!

SAINT PATRICK.

Torn away by pirates, tending in a strange land a heathen master's swine, the slave boy, with the spirit of Christ in his heart, praying in the snow for those who had enslaved him, and returning to bring to his oppressors the message of the Gospel, returning with good to give where evil had been received, to kindle in the darkness a great light—this is Ireland's patron saint. In his spirit let Ireland's struggle be. Not merely through Irish vales and hamlets, but into England, into Scotland, into Wales, wherever the English tongue is spoken, let the torch be carried and the word be preached. And beyond! The brotherhood of man stops not with differences of speech any more than with seas or mountain chains. A century ago it was ours to speak the ringing word. Then it was France's. Now it may be Ireland's, if her sons be true.

THE WORK MUST BE DONE.

But wherever, or by whom, the word must be spoken, the standard will be raised. No matter what the Irish leaders do or do not do, it is too late to permanently settle the question on any basis short of the recognition of equal natural rights. And, whether the Land Leagues move forward or slink back, the agitation must spread to this side of the Atlantic. The Republic, the *true* Republic, is not yet here. But her birth struggle must soon begin. Already, with the hope of her, men's thoughts are stirring.

Not a republic of landlords and peasants; not a republic of millionaires and tramps; not a republic in which some are masters and some serve. But a republic of equal citizens, where competition becomes co-operation, and the interdependence of all gives true independence to each; where moral progress goes hand-in-hand with intellectual progress, and material progress elevates and enfranchises even the poorest and weakest and lowliest.

ALL TO RECEIVE THEIR GOD-GIVEN RIGHTS.

And the gospel of deliverance, let us not forget it; it is the gospel of love, not of hate. He whom it emancipates will know neither Jew nor Gentile, nor Irishman nor Englishman, nor German nor Frenchman, nor European nor American, nor difference of colour nor of race, nor animosities of class nor condition. Let us set our feet on old prejudices, let us bury the old hates. There have been "Holy Alliances" of kings. Let us strive for the Holy Alliance of the people.

Liberty, equality, fraternity! Write them on the banners. Let them be for sign and countersign. Without equality, liberty cannot be; without fraternity, neither equality nor liberty can be achieved.

Liberty—the full freedom of each bounded only by the equal freedom of every other.

Equality—the equal right of each to the use and enjoyment of all natural opportunities, to all the essentials of happy, healthful, human life!

Fraternity—that sympathy which links together those who struggle in a noble cause; that would live and let live; that would help as well as be helped; that, in seeking the good of all, finds the highest good of each!

"By this sign shall ye conquer!"

"*We hold these truths to be self-evident: That all men are created equal; that they are endowed by their Creator with certain unalienable rights; that among these are life, liberty, and the pursuit of happiness!*"

It is over a century since these words rang out. It is time to give them their full, true meaning. Let the standard be lifted that all may see it; let the advance be sounded that all may hear it. Let those who would fall back, fall back. Let those who would oppose, oppose. Everywhere are those who will rally. The stars in their courses fight against Sisera!

HENRY GEORGE.

NEW YORK, *March, 1881.*

DUNN AND WRIGHT, PRINTERS, GLASGOW.

Made in United States
Troutdale, OR
11/03/2026

56844446R00040